SCHOLASTIC

Grade 1
Writing Curriculum:
Week-by-Week Lessons

BY KATHLEEN A. CARDEN AND MARY GODLEY-SUGRUE

NEW YORK • TORONTO • LONDON • AUCKLAND • SYDNEY
MEXICO CITY • NEW DELHI • HONG KONG • BUENOS AIRES

Teaching *Resources*

Dedication:

Dedicated to my husband Tom, and my children, Tommy, Meghan, Patrick, William, and Jack for giving me the love, support, and countless hours necessary to make this book a reality. —K.C.

To my children Anne Marie and Jimmy, who are just beginning to blossom as writers, and to developing writers everywhere. May they always cherish the creativity and self-expression achieved through writing. —M.S.

Acknowledgments:

Special thanks to my parents, Jack and Dorothy Whalen for making sacrifices to ensure quality education throughout my life; to my friend and mentor, Margo Turner, who shared her work ethic and taught me how to teach; to my co-author, Mary Sugrue, for sharing her knowledge and ideas with me; and to my editor, Joanna Davis-Swing for her gentle guidance throughout this writing process. —K.C.

Many thanks to all who helped to make these books come alive with their ongoing encouragement and babysitting: the grandparents—Brigid and Richard Godley, Mary and Bartholomew Sugrue, my husband Jim, my former colleagues at Goudy School and principal Mr. Durkin, and our editor Joanna Davis-Swing. —M.S.

Scholastic Inc. grants teachers permission to photocopy the reproducible pages in this book for classroom use. No other part of this publication may be reproduced in whole or in part, or stored in a retrieval system, or transmitted in any form or by any means, electronic, mechanical, photocopying, recording, or otherwise, without written permission of the publisher. For information regarding permission, write to Scholastic Inc., 557 Broadway, New York, NY 10012.

Cover design by Maria Lilja
Interior design by Holly Grundon
Interior illustrations by Milk and Cookies

ISBN: 0-439-52982-4

Copyright © 2005 by Kathleen A. Carden and Mary Godley-Sugrue
All rights reserved. Published by Scholastic Inc.
Printed in the U.S.A.

4 5 6 7 8 9 10   40   11 10 09 08 07

Contents

Introduction

This book is written for all teachers, administrators, and parents who would like to see their students become confident, capable writers. We know how vital this is for success in the academic world and beyond, yet too often we fail students by not providing the direct instruction and guided practice they need to develop as writers. Low test scores and poor performance are the all-too-common result: 42% of Illinois third graders tested did not meet the writing standards (*Chicago Tribune*, 15 Nov. 2001, sec. 1:28). In 2002 the bad news continued, with the headlines reading: "Poor Scores for Writing Alarms State" (*Chicago Tribune*, 4 Aug. 2002, sec. 1:1). This tale is also true of New York third graders. "Despite last minute infusion of $8 million to prepare students for tests, 11,700 of city public school system's 80,000 third graders scored in the lowest of four categories . . . putting them below cutoff for promotion and in danger of being held back" (*New York Times*, 4 June 2004, sec. A). Across the country in California, we find the same concerns: " . . . Writing Skill Lagging in Grade 4, 8; A national test puts California in the bottom third of states, with just 23% of youngsters in those grades rating proficient or advanced" (*Los Angeles Times*, 11 July 2003, sec. B:8). These writing woes are spread from coast to coast and have serious implications for our nation as a whole.

The National Writing Commission has addressed this issue in their April 2003 report, "The Neglected 'R': The Need for a Writing Revolution." The report notes that "American education will never realize its potential as an engine of opportunity and economic growth until a writing revolution puts language and communication in their proper place in the classroom." We agree. As educators with 25 years of experience between us, we have seen firsthand the need for a comprehensive writing curriculum to address this problem. The writing curriculum should include direct instruction, teacher modeling, guided practice, conferring, and the use of consistent terminology across grade levels. In addition, there needs to be continuity among the grade levels so that the skill of writing sentences is mastered before paragraph formation, and paragraph formation is mastered before essay writing.

This is book one of a three-book series in which writing skills are sequentially taught. Book one (typically for first graders) works on sentence writing and builds up to paragraph writing. Book two (typically for second graders) reinforces paragraph writing and moves on to simple essay writing with introductions and conclusions. Book three (typically for third graders) works on multiple-paragraph essays and prepares students for taking the state writing exams.

Writing is about communicating. It is the art of expressing feelings, emotions, ideas, and information on paper. As first-grade teachers, you want to create an enthusiasm for writing that will be nurtured and developed throughout your students' schooling experience. You want your students to feel comfortable, confident, and secure enough to want to express their thoughts on paper. What's more you want to provide them with lots of opportunities to be successful. Instead of drills, you can use mini-lessons to teach and to reinforce skills. These quick lessons can be followed by plenty of practice. It is the love of writing that will be almost impossible to instill if too much "skill and drill" bogs students down in the early years.

We have walked in your shoes, hunting and pecking through a multitude of writing books in search of the perfect writing lessons. We hope that you find our collection of journal prompts, weekly lessons, and reproducible planning pages helpful. Use the ones that work for you and adapt the others to your needs. By following our program of Daily Journal Prompts and Weekly Writing Instruction, your students will be on their way to writing proficiently.

First-Grade Writers

A Developmental Portrait

Gather a group of first graders and ask them: "When did you learn how to ride a two-wheeler?" You may get one or two students who tell you that they learned at the age of three. A few more will proudly state that they learned at age four. Still others will say five was the magic age. In addition, a couple of brave souls will admit that they are still trying to master this developmental milestone.

The writing development of your first graders, in many respects, parallels the bike-riding experience. You can expect to see a wide span of experience and abilities. A handful of your students will have been writing stories and filling up notebook pages with near-perfect spelling since kindergarten. Others will barely be writing their names. The reason for this broad range of ability is the varying amounts of exposure to writing across kindergarten curriculums, as well as varying student development levels at this age. This chapter provides an overview of the typical developmental stages most first graders go through. Then we share the curriculum we developed in response to first graders' needs and the standards they are expected to meet by the end of the year.

Developmental Stages of Beginning Writers

When looking at first-grade writing in September and again in June, you will see that the growth span is unbelievable. But to get where they are in June, students have to start somewhere. And "somewhere" includes learning to spell, learning conventions of print (including spatial awareness and punctuation), and learning to organize thoughts.

STAGES OF SPELLING DEVELOPMENT

Spelling is a challenge to first-grade writers. We encourage students to use invented spelling when they write so they don't spend all of their writing time worrying about how to spell words correctly. Invented spelling is valuable for many reasons. It reinforces phonics skills by encouraging students to match sounds to letters. As they get used to doing this, they begin to focus on letters and print found elsewhere—in the classroom and in books. Hence, students make the connection between reading and writing early, and their gains in one area transfer to the other. Invented spelling also takes the emphasis away from perfection, allowing students to take risks and focus on the purpose of their writing. Students who are not encouraged to use invented spelling often simplify their ideas to include only words that they are confident they can spell.

In addition, it is important to understand how children learn to spell. Spelling is a developmental process, with students passing through predictable stages as their spelling develops. Every student is different, and therefore will pass through each stage at different rates. Within a first-grade classroom, you are more than likely going to have students functioning at all stages of development. Following are descriptions of the stages often seen in first-grade classrooms, as defined by J. Richard Gentry and Jean Wallace Gillet (1993).

Prephonetic Stage

The first stage of spelling development is the prephonetic stage. At this point, students do not have the knowledge of phonics and therefore do not know that letters represent sounds. They may be excited to write, however, and may busy themselves by filling up pages with random strings of letters, pictures, or numbers. They may even try to copy written language around them, such as signs and posters in the classroom. Most students generally pass through this stage in kindergarten, but you may see some students entering first grade at this stage.

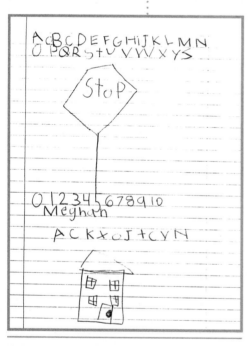

Sample of student writing in the prephonetic stage.

Semiphonetic Stage

The next stage, the semiphonetic stage, begins with students using single letters to represent words. For example, students at this stage may draw a picture of a dog and a cat, and then write *D* and *K* under it.

Phonetic Stage

As they broaden their knowledge of phonetics, students enter the phonetic stage. Here they begin to spell words according to the way they sound. Beginning and ending consonant sounds become more accurate, but students confuse vowels and vowel patterns. Spellings are becoming decodable due to the accuracy of consonant sounds.

Students in the phonetic stage, probably the majority of your class at the beginning of the year, will enjoy writing messages and creating lists, signs, sentences, and simple stories. As you create a print-rich environment in your classroom, allow students to label items, write lists, and make signs (No Boys Allowed/No Girls Allowed are two popular ones that you'll have to veto right away!). By encouraging these activities throughout the day, you are creating purpose and enthusiasm for writing.

Transitional Stage

Next, students pass through the transitional stage, a bridge from phonetic to conventional spelling. At this stage, students begin to spell words as they "look" rather than as they "sound." Students' spellings begin to look very close to actual, or conventional, spelling.

Through reading, transitional spellers also learn conventions of the English language, such as vowel patterns and digraphs, and they begin to try them out in their own spellings. You may want to post a list of commonly misspelled words, which students

Sample of student writing in the semiphonetic stage

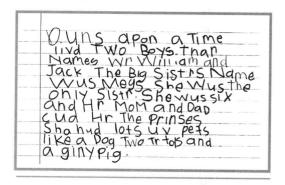

Sample of student writing in the transitional stage

Sample of student writing in the phonetic stage

Sample of student writing in the transitional stage

can refer to, especially in this stage. By the end of first grade, most of your students will be in this stage.

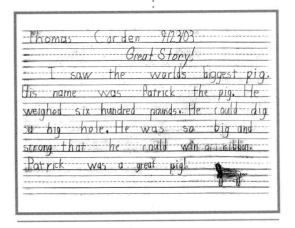

Sample of student writing in the conventional stage

Name:_____
Weekly Spelling List
Unit _____
1._____
2._____
3._____
4._____
5._____
6._____
7._____
8._____
9._____
10._____

Sample form for weekly spelling words. After a pretest of the book list, students copy only the words that they misspelled. They then find (with your help) additional words from their journal and writing projects to complete the weekly list.

Conventional Stage

Finally, students enter the conventional stage of spelling. It is in this stage that students will tell you they can "spell like adults." Their spellings are correct, and they will use a dictionary to find the spellings of any unknown words. Just as with the first stage, you can only expect to see a couple of first-grade writers spelling at this stage.

Where Does My Spelling Program Fit In?

Your school or district will most likely have a spelling program in place that you will be required to use. While spelling programs provide practice and instruction, we believe that students will ultimately learn to spell from engaging in meaningful writing activities.

To make the most of a spelling series, we recommend giving a pretest to determine which words students know at the beginning of the week. Then, to personalize spelling instruction, have students copy only the words they did not know how to spell onto their weekly list. Supplement the list with unknown words from a high-frequency list (such as the Dolch list) as well as their journal entries and weekly writing assignments. You can make a form similar to the one at left.

Encouraging invented spelling and providing purposeful writing (which you will find plenty of in this book) are the keys to teaching students to spell. Do not be afraid to print the word yourself above a word written by a phonetic writer to make it easier to read, or to send a transitional writer to a dictionary if he or she is at your desk continuously because a word doesn't "look right."

PRINT CONVENTIONS

During shared reading, guided reading, and other instructional activities, first graders discover that there are certain rules, or conventions, required to make print "work." They have learned that letters must be arranged in a certain order to form words. Now they will become aware that spaces separate words and periods separate sentences. As students acquire these concepts about print, we help them apply them to their own writing.

Spatial Awareness

One convention that first graders will learn is that spaces separate words. As students develop this spatial awareness of print, some will take it upon themselves to use large lines or dots, rather than spaces, between each word. For example, I/went/to/Disney/World/over/the/summer/and/I/saw/Mickey/Mouse; I*like*to*play*school.

This spacing technique will pass quickly. You can help by calling attention to proper spacing as you model writing conventions and pointing out spacing in books while reading. Also, use the finger-space rule: one finger space between words and two finger spaces between sentences.

Punctuation

Another convention that first graders need to master is ending punctuation. Just as spaces separate words, periods separate sentences. Periods are the stop signs that tell us to stop reading because an idea is over. Without them the writing will not make sense to the reader. Read some sample sentences without pausing to illustrate the importance of ending punctuation.

GENERATING AND ORGANIZING IDEAS

When first graders are asked to write a story, many of them shy away. It seems to be a risk that many are reluctant to take. They may ask, "What should I write about?" or "What if my story doesn't make sense?" Young writers need a great deal of help generating and organizing their thoughts at first. At the beginning, students will be more comfortable drawing a picture and labeling it. Next, they will move on to drawing a picture and writing a simple sentence. Finally, with the help of your modeling and conferring, they advance to writing a group of sentences to explain their idea.

Since many students will need assistance generating and organizing ideas, this book provides templates to assist with organizing thoughts. In addition,

Allow students to self-correct spelling tests, or point out a misspelled high-frequency word during a conference, and have students correct it so they can visualize their error.

we suggest lots of brainstorming and teacher modeling. Initially, students will brainstorm pictorially and then use their illustrations as a springboard for their written work. Later, most students will move on to a written brainstorm. Each assignment provides a planning page with ample brainstorming space to generate and organize ideas.

You will find that writing assignments in this book follow a process approach to teaching writing, and that even your most reluctant writers will be more apt to give writing a try with the support of a structured, predictable framework. The consistent use of the writing process (analyzing the audience, setting the purpose, brainstorming, drafting, conferring, editing, revising, and sharing) will allow students to feel in control at each step along the way. Your modeling of the writing process paired with our sequenced assignments will give young writers the tools they need to generate and organize their own ideas, and to build their confidence to become independent writers by the end of the year.

TIP

If a student is having a hard time remembering to use ending punctuation, have the student first say, then write, and finally stop the sentence by using a red marker or a red star sticker to symbolize a stop sign. Continue with this visual approach until the student has internalized the rule.

CHAPTER 2

First-Grade Writers

A Curriculum

TIP

To become competent writers, students must have ample time to practice writing every day, coupled with direct instruction on specific skills and conventions. With time and teaching, first graders will progress as writers along the developmental continuum described in the last chapter. This chapter describes the curriculum we have developed over the years to teach first-grade writers.

Our curriculum has two main components: daily journal writing and a weekly writing lesson, which consists of direct instruction, guided practice, independent work, conferring, and sharing. The journal prompts and writing lessons are arranged according to the academic calendar. The writing lessons cover narrative, expository, and persuasive genres, as well as letter, short story, and poetry writing. It is our goal to provide clear descriptions and consistent terminology, so that all teachers and students will feel comfortable with the writing process.

At times, the writing instruction may seem highly directive, but remember that children need training wheels to get the basic form prior to riding a two-wheeler on their own. Students will pass through the developmental stages of spelling and develop their knowledge of print conventions at different rates, just as they will take off their training wheels at different times. It is important to know that, just as in riding a two-wheeler, they will all get to the same point eventually. Our open-ended topics allow students to respond creatively at their own level of development. The reproducible pages guide students through the weekly lesson, yet allow them to respond in their own voice, avoiding the recipe-like, contrived writing of which the scorers of many state writing exams have been critical. The weekly writing instruction pages include the genre, skill, standard, assignment, focus, model, and a conferring tip for each assignment; see the overview of assignments and skills on pages 14–15. The rest of this chapter describes our writing curriculum in detail.

TIP

All of the writing assignments should be completed in class to ensure student-generated work. If these assignments are homework, parents may intervene. By keeping the assignments in class, you are also ensuring weekly student writing. Remember that ultimately the students learn to write by writing, not by listening about how to write.

Assignment	Genre	Skill(s)	Standard(s)
Classroom Rules (p. 42)	Expository sentences	Capitalizing the beginning of sentences	Use correct grammar, spelling, punctuation, capitalization, and structure.
A Summer Memory (p. 44)	Narrative sentences	Using ending punctuation: period	Use correct grammar, spelling, punctuation, capitalization, and structure.
Getting to Know You, Part I (p. 46)	Interrogatory sentences	Using ending punctuation: question mark	Use correct grammar, spelling, punctuation, capitalization, and structure.
Getting to Know You, Part II (p. 48)	Descriptive sentences	Writing answers to questions; presenting information	Apply acquired information to communicate in a variety of formats. Speak effectively using appropriate language.
Surprise Bag (p. 50)	Descriptive sentences	Using descriptive language	Present brief oral reports, using language and vocabulary appropriate to the message and audience.
Special Me (p. 56)	Descriptive sentences	Avoiding redundancy	Compose well-organized and coherent writing.
The Best Game (p. 58)	Persuasive sentences	Persuading the audience	Communicate ideas in writing to accomplish a variety of purposes.
Halloween Costumes (p. 60)	Descriptive sentences	Using descriptive language	Compose well-organized and coherent writing for specific purposes and audiences.
A Hobby of Mine (p. 62)	Expository sentences	Using time-order transitions	Use correct grammar, spelling, punctuation, capitalization, and structure.
Lunchtime (p. 68)	Lists	Arranging items in order	Communicate ideas in writing to accomplish a variety of purposes.
I Am Thankful (p. 70)	Friendly letter	Using correct capitalization and punctuation in greetings and closings	Communicate ideas in writing to accomplish a variety of purposes. Use correct grammar, spelling, punctuation, capitalization, and structure.
Making a Turkey (p. 72)	Expository sentences	Writing directions	Write for a variety of purposes, including description, information, explanation, persuasion, and narration.
You'll Never Believe What Came Alive! (p. 74)	Narrative sentences	Sequencing events in a story	Use prewriting strategies to generate and organize ideas (e.g., focus on one topic; organize writing to include a beginning, middle, and end; use descriptive words when writing about people, places, things, events), and write for a variety of purposes.
How to Build a Snowman (p. 79)	Expository sentences	Using time-order transitions	Write for a variety of purposes, including description, information, explanation, persuasion, and narration.
My Favorite Place (p. 81)	Descriptive sentences	Using sensory language	Use prewriting strategies to generate and organize ideas (e.g., focus on one topic; organize writing to include a beginning, middle, and end; use descriptive words when writing about people, places, things, and events).
To Have or Not to Have . . . Cable TV (p. 83)	Persuasive sentences	Persuading the audience	Write for a variety of purposes, including persuasion.
Winter Vacation (p. 88)	Narrative paragraph	Writing paragraphs	Communicate ideas in writing to accomplish a variety of purposes.

Assignment	Genre	Skill(s)	Standard(s)
My Good Friend (p. 91)	Descriptive paragraph	Using START to expand brainstorm ideas and write a paragraph	Use prewriting strategies to generate and organize ideas (e.g., focus on one topic; organize writing to include a beginning, middle, and end; use descriptive words when writing about people, places, things, and events).
Thank You, Thank You! (p. 94)	Thank-you letter	Using parts of a letter—greeting, body, and closing	Communicate ideas in writing to accomplish a variety of purposes. Use correct grammar, spelling, punctuation, capitalization, and structure.
Dear Visitor (p. 100)	Formal letter	Using parts of a letter—greeting, body, and closing	Write letters, reports, and stories based on acquired information. Compose well-organized and coherent writing for specific purposes and audiences.
My Invention (p. 102)	Expository paragraph	Using elaboration	Demonstrate focus, organization, elaboration, and integration in written compositions.
School Fun (p. 104)	Narrative paragraph	Writing paragraphs—purpose, supporting sentences, and sentences of elaboration	Communicate ideas in writing to accomplish a variety of purposes. Demonstrate focus, organization, and elaboration in writing.
Something I Do Well (p. 106)	Narrative paragraph	Writing compound sentences	Use correct grammar, spelling, punctuation, and capitalization.
Dear Teacher (p. 112)	Persuasive letter	Writing supporting sentences	Write letters, reports, and stories based on acquired information.
My Favorite Toy (p. 114)	Descriptive paragraph	Using descriptive language (similes)	Communicate ideas in writing to accomplish a variety of purposes.
The Best Day of My Life (p. 116)	Narrative paragraph	Sequencing and using time-order transitions	Relate character, setting, and plot to real-life situations.
Following the Rainbow (p. 118)	Fiction	Sequencing—beginning, middle, and end	Use prewriting strategies to generate and organize ideas (e.g., focus on one topic; organize writing to include a beginning, middle, and end; use descriptive words when writing about people, places, things, and events).
Indoor vs. Outdoor Recess (p. 123)	Persuasive paragraph	Writing supporting sentences	Demonstrate focus, organization, and elaboration in writing. Write for a variety of purposes.
Rainy-Day Fun (p. 125)	Expository paragraph	Using time-order transitions	Communicate ideas in writing to accomplish a variety of purposes.
Who Let the Dog Out? (p. 127)	Fiction	Using rich vocabulary	Relate character, setting, and plot to real-life situations.
Taking Care of a Pet (p. 133)	Expository paragraph	Editing/revising	Use correct grammar, spelling, punctuation, capitalization, and structure.
When I Was a Baby (p. 135)	Narrative paragraph	Understanding subject-verb agreement and past-tense verb formation	Use correct grammar, spelling, punctuation, capitalization, and structure.
Earning a Privilege (p. 138)	Persuasive paragraph	Choosing titles	Communicate ideas in writing to accomplish a variety of purposes.
A New Take on an Old Story (p. 140)	Fiction	Using dialogue	Identify how author and illustrators express their ideas.
Acrostic Poem (p. 145)	Poetry	Using descriptive language	Describe differences between prose and poetry.
Name Poem (p. 148)	Poetry	Rhyming words	Communicate ideas in writing to accomplish a variety of purposes.
Cinquain (p. 151)	Poetry	Using descriptive language	Communicate ideas in writing to accomplish a variety of purposes.

Daily Journal Writing

Daily journal time should be a fun free-writing experience that helps students enjoy writing as they practice generating and expressing ideas. We provide you with daily journal prompts that relate to the season as well as topics of interest to first graders. Remember that these are just suggestions. Allow students the opportunity to make their journals meaningful by writing on topics of their own choice. You may also wish to substitute prompts that are specific to related curriculum.

In addition to daily journals, many teachers use math, science, and/or literature response journals as a tool for students to demonstrate their knowledge of subject matter, as well as to practice their writing skills. Writing across the curriculum ensures that students not only get more practice but also see the importance of writing in their daily lives—that they are writing for a wide variety of purposes. The more students have the opportunity to write, the better they will become at it, so never pass up an opportunity for students to use written language.

ESTABLISHING THE ROUTINE AND SETTING EXPECTATIONS

For journaling to be the most effective, you'll need to establish a regular time for it each day. Students should write in their journals for about ten minutes every day (including illustrating time). Many teachers prefer to use the first ten minutes of the morning. Others like to get students started and then use it as independent work while they meet with small groups of students. Still others prefer to journal right after the lunch and recess break, as a way of calming and focusing the students for the afternoon. We recommend that you write along with the students and share your responses with them. This is a wonderful way for students to get to know you on a personal level. The hardest thing initially is finding the time. Once you achieve that, you will see how quickly it becomes a routine that students look forward to each day.

You'll also need to establish your expectations for the journal and journaling time so everyone is clear on what to do. Decide on your criteria and then teach them to students. You may need to model the process and illustrate your expectations more than once. We find the following supplies essential and require all students to have them ready at the beginning of journal time:

A journal notebook: Spiral notebooks are the easiest to use, but the lines may be intimidating to some beginning writers. Primary journals (lots of picture space and primary printing lines) can be purchased through school supply stores, but can be costly. You may choose to make your own journals by stapling sheets of 8 1/2-by-11-inch paper with a few writing lines and a lot of picture space in between two pieces of colored construction paper. As students gain confidence, you can add more printing lines and thus decrease the amount of picture space. When students appear ready, they can transition to a spiral notebook.

Pencils and erasers: All writing should be done in pencil so that students can easily make changes during the writing process. Rewriting an entire piece not only creates unnecessary frustration, but also destroys enthusiasm for the project. Standard erasers often break off the pencil tops, so we recommend using cap erasers that can be slipped on.

Primary paper with space for illustrations

Once students have their supplies ready, the next step is to date the page. The journal is an important tool that shows growth over the course of the school year, and students should be encouraged to look back at their work periodically. The date can be written by the student, or stamped by the student using a rubber date stamp. Next, students should focus their attention on you as you introduce the prompt. You can write it on the chalkboard, chart paper, or overhead projector. It is important to read through the daily prompt and then discuss and elaborate to ensure that all students understand and are able to respond.

The prompt generally ends with a question for the students to answer. Often students have a hard time incorporating the prompt question into their response. To help students develop this ability, we include sentence starters with the prompts (see the examples below). This will help students begin their writing with a purpose, or main idea, a skill necessary for success on future writing exams.

What would you like to be when you grow up and why?

When I grow up, I'd like to be a

_____ .

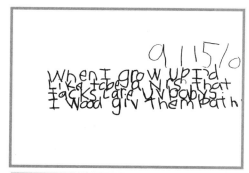

Sample journal entry written by a first grader

Sample journal entry from a beginning writer

Sample journal entry from a more advanced writer

After you've introduced and discussed the prompt, students then copy the sentence starter into their journals and begin to write.

Each journal entry should be a minimum of one to two sentences at the beginning of the year, working up to five by the end of the year. This count includes the sentence starter. Five sentences may seem like a lot, but it is always better to have high expectations so that the students will aim high. Even if they fall short of their goal, their results will still be impressive. For struggling or beginning writers, you may need to adjust your expectations. Perhaps drawing a picture and labeling it, or writing one sentence, is more reasonable for a struggling writer. On the other hand, a more advanced writer might be expected to elaborate more and thus write more sentences.

You may have to walk around the room to ensure that students are complying with the length requirement. They often confuse three, four, or five sentences with three, four, or five lines.

ENCOURAGING RESPONSE

Allow students time to illustrate their journal entries with crayons, markers, or colored pencils. These illustrations will help develop descriptive language as the year progresses. It may be easier for some students to illustrate their response to a prompt and then use words to tell about it. Students are apt to describe things more vividly with words when they are also planning their illustrations. The illustrations also help beginning writers develop confidence, as they too can feel proud about having something on their page.

Another way to motivate writers is to let them use the computer. If your school is like many, the computer time and number of computers is limited. However, journals are a great writing assignment for the computer because they are short, so students can practice with computer-generated writing and related components, such as typing, spell check, and the thesaurus. You may wish to post a schedule so that students can see when they will be able to use the computer for their journal time.

Managing and Assessing Journals

When you are finished journaling, and as the students are still writing, walk around the room to monitor their progress and offer individualized help. Aim to work with about one-fifth of the class each day. This will save you from having to collect the entire set of journals at the end of the week.

Always write a comment or a question, as students love to read teacher feedback. Keep this feedback informal and positive during the free-writing journal activity.

Allow a few student volunteers to share their journal entries with the class at the end of journal time. Never force students to read an entry if they are not yet comfortable doing so, but we've found that first graders are usually eager to share. There may be a few who are reluctant, but once they see the positive feedback that the presenter receives, they too will soon be eager to share their work. Once everyone is eager to share and/or when the writing gets longer, you may wish to make a schedule to ensure that all students have an equal opportunity to present their work. Sit near the writer in case he or she needs assistance reading. You may need to rewrite a word or two above younger writers' words so that it can be reread easily.

Ask students to accept three questions or comments from the audience. Make sure that, beginning with the first sharing session, you model your questions or comments first. Always start with a positive comment and/or question such as the following:

> I like how you gave examples of your favorite gym games. I was wondering how you play Dr. Dodgeball.

> I like how you shared that your favorite animal was the polar bear. I was wondering what it is that you liked so much about him.

At the end of every month, invite students to choose one entry that they think shows their best work. This will allow the students some responsibility for self-assessment, as well as keeping you from having to read all of the journals every day. The grading should be holistic, evaluating length, creativity, and effort. Do not get caught up in grammar and style—just write a comment about your overall impression. Try to avoid marking up young

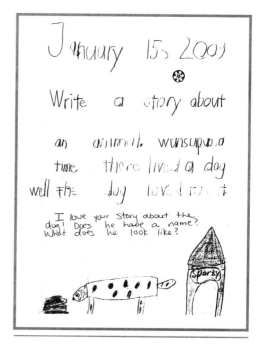

Sample journal entry with teacher comments

TIP

Use a checklist to make sure that you have read something from each student each week, and to record any words that you think students should add to their personalized spelling lists.

writers' "masterpieces" with a lot of red marks. This can deflate their confidence, and, as a result, can turn them off writing. Use positive comments to reward them for their successes, and offer gentle suggestions to guide them through their obstacles. Remember—the nature of journaling is free writing.

Weekly Writing Instruction

We have developed a five-day lesson that teaches an important writing skill and gives students the opportunity to practice using the skill as they take a piece through the writing process. Here is an overview of our lesson sequence.

Day 1: **Teach Skill/Assign Topic/Prewriting**
Students:
- *analyze audience*
- *set purpose*
- *brainstorm ideas*

Day 2: **Drafting**
Students:
- *talk with peer: two-minute chat*
- *complete planning page*
- *begin drafting*

Day 3: **Drafting/Revising/Conferring**
Students:
- *complete drafting*
- *begin revising*
- *confer with teacher*

Day 4: **Revising/Editing/Conferring**
Students:
- *finish revising*
- *edit work*
- *confer with teacher*

Day 5: **Sharing**
Students:
- *prepare work for sharing*
- *share*

The weekly writing lessons allow students the opportunity to practice many types of writing under your direction. It is here that the steps of the writing process, as well as individual skills, are taught. You will need to set aside 20 to 30 minutes per day to work on the lesson. The lessons address genre, skills, and standards, and they invite you to model, using the planning page and conferring tips. (For a detailed walk-through of a weekly lesson, see pages 22–25.)

We encourage you to write along with the students. This writing can take place during journal time, weekly mini-lessons, drafting, or conferring. You may wish to model on the overhead projector because it is easy to view, and it provides ample space for writing and editing. Other places for you to model writing include chart paper and the chalkboard. Do not fear crossing out, changing, adding, and so on because this is all part of the writing process, and it is good for the students to see that even adult writers have to work to make the writing flow.

TOOLS NEEDED FOR WEEKLY WRITING LESSONS

Each student needs to have a working folder in his or her desk for "work in progress." This working folder should have a list of commonly misspelled words and/or high-frequency writing words, a planning page for the current assignment (which we include with each lesson), and START and STOP reminder sheets after these tools have been taught (see pages 28–29). Once paragraph writing is introduced in January, a list of transitional words should also be placed in this folder.

Each student should also have a permanent writing folder, which can be part of an assessment portfolio. This folder is a great resource to track student growth. All prewriting and draft work can be saved and stapled under the final product. This permanent file should be kept in the your file cabinet. Take the folders out periodically and share them with students so they can look back and see their growth. Make sure that the students know it is normal to see some "silly" things from the beginning of the year and that they should be proud of how much they've grown. Without this reassurance, many first graders will look back at their work and erase errors because they now "know better."

TIP

When children read or listen to their favorite book, they do not realize all of the revisions that the author has made to the story. If your school or PTA/PTO arranges visits from local authors as part of students' enrichment, be sure to ask the author(s) to share their writing experiences with the students. (Many authors will tell students that by the time their book was finished, they could not recognize their original idea(s).)

Sample Weekly Writing
Lesson and Schedule

WEEK 1 LESSON: CLASSROOM RULES

DAY 1 . . .

On the first day, you'll introduce the assignment, building students' interest in the topic and motivating them to write. You'll walk students through the first steps on the planning page, a reproducible student page used to generate and organize ideas. For Lesson 1, you might begin like this:

Teacher: Today we're going to talk about rules. It seems like there are lots and lots of rules we have to follow, both at home and at school, and other places, too. Who can tell us some rules they have to follow?

Student: I always have to wash my hands before dinner.

Student: I have to do my homework before I watch TV.

Student: I'm not allowed to hit my little brother.

Teacher: Well, those do sound like good rules to me. Would the rest of you agree? (*Students nod their heads.*)

Students: I have to do those things too.

Student: Yeah, without the rule about homework before TV, I might not finish it.

Teacher: So rules help us do things we have to do, things that are good for us. They are important, even though we might not like them sometimes.

Today we're going to think about rules that would help us work together in the classroom. Then we're going to write about our rule and why we think it's important.

At this point, distribute the planning page that goes with the lesson. Discuss who the audience is—in this case, you and students' peers. Then help students set their purpose. This requires choosing a rule, so invite discussion about possible rules and record them on chart paper, the overhead, or the chalkboard. After you've collected many examples, model how you turn the brainstormed ideas into sentences, being sure to point out that you capitalize the first word of each sentence—this is the writing convention being taught in this lesson. You might say:

Teacher: William suggested that we should not run in the classroom because someone could fall and hit his head. That's a very important rule. I will need to start my sentence with a capital letter, so I'll make a capital D and write: "Do not run in the classroom."

Model several sentences in this fashion, reminding students that a sentence always begins with a capital letter. At the end of this part of the lesson, ask a student volunteer to highlight or underline all of the beginning capital letters in your sentences. Reread the examples as a group, making sure that all students are watching so that they can make a visual connection to this capitalization rule. Also, emphasize the importance of capitalization as a signal to the audience or reader that a new sentence is beginning.

After your demonstration, invite students to choose a rule they think is important and write it in the purpose statement on the planning page. The next step is to brainstorm support for the purpose statement. In this case, students are asked to illustrate the rule. As students gain more experience, they may begin to brainstorm in words, but at first, drawings help them capture their ideas more effectively. When they finish drawing, ask them to write three words about their idea in the space provided. You can provide support as needed.

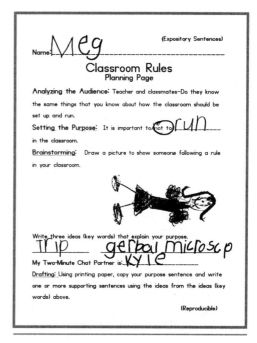

Sample planning page

DAY 2 . . .

Review the work done the previous day and have students read over their planning pages.

Two-Minute Chat: Now students have a chance to discuss their ideas with a partner. Have each partner present his or her purpose statement, drawing, and words. Encourage partners to ask questions. You will have to model this skill many times. For instance, for the planning page above, you might say:

Teacher:	Hmm, I see that Meg is concerned about the gerbil and microscope, but I'm not sure how this connects to the rule of no running. Why did you mention the gerbil and the microscope?
Meg:	Well, if you run you might trip and fall and break something. The microscope might smash into pieces, and then we couldn't use it anymore.
Teacher:	"Smash into pieces" really helps me picture what might happen if someone were to run in the classroom. Those are very descriptive words.

This step helps students focus their ideas and generate more words to describe them. It is important because the verbal skills of first graders are often more sophisticated than their written skills; they will often elaborate on their brainstorm when given the opportunity to verbalize their thoughts.

Drafting: After the two-minute chat, call students together and tell them it's time to begin writing. For the first few lessons, you will want to model how you use the keywords to write sentences from your own planning page. After some brief modeling, invite students to begin by writing their purpose statement on a sheet of loose-leaf or lined printing paper. Encourage them to use their key words in their writing and to remember what they discussed with their partner.

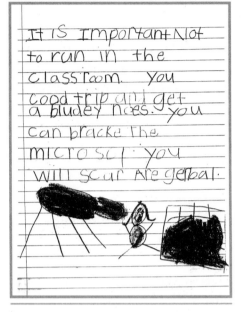

Sample draft from an advanced first-grade writer

You should expect and encourage invented spelling. You may ask students to read their sentences to you while you print the word above any words that cannot be easily decoded so you (and the student!) can read it again later. Most students will probably begin each sentence with the same word, as in the example above. You will work on this later when you teach paragraph writing. Remember that for now you are trying to instill an enthusiasm for writing; enthusiastically accept all students' efforts.

A t the beginning of the year you may need to take dictation from "younger" writers.

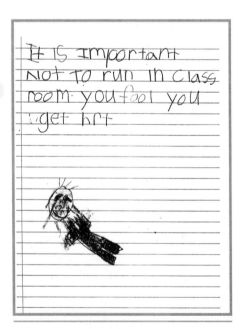

Sample draft from a developing first-grade writer

Sample draft from a beginning first-grade writer

Conferring: As students finish drafting their sentences, you'll want to confer with them. You can do this one-on-one or in small groups of no more than three students. Each lesson has a conferring tip. In this lesson, the focus is on capitalizing the first word of a sentence, so you may want to address this skill in conference if students are having a hard time with it. (See page 31 for more ideas on conferring.)

DAY 3 . . .

Have students review their planning pages and drafting from the previous day and ask them to continue drafting if necessary, or to begin editing and revising once they've met with you.

Editing/Revising: Later in the year, students will use STOP (see page 29) to edit and revise their work independently. For now, review the beginning capitalization that you discussed on Day 1. Students should be looking to see that they began their sentence(s) with a capital letter. Continue conferring with students.

Those who have finished drafting and are waiting for a conference can illustrate their piece, read it to a friend who is also finished, or help a classmate who is still drafting.

DAY 4 . . .

Finish editing/revising/conferring.

DAY 5 . . .

Sharing: Allow students the chance to sit in the "Author" chair and present their work to the class. (See a detailed description of sharing, beginning on page 30.) You will probably be able to finish all of the pieces in one sitting, as they are not very lengthy at this point.

At the end of class, collect all work, date it and label it as the first assignment, and store it in students' portfolios.

The Writing Curriculum and the Writing Process

Writing is a process, much like cooking. While the goal of each process is something tangible prepared for an audience—an editorial, perhaps, or a birthday cake—the processes themselves differ in an important way. A chef must follow the steps in a recipe sequentially, or the end result may not be edible. But the writing process is cyclical. If the piece is not flowing or making sense, writers can go back and redo steps, and, if necessary, start over. The steps to the writing process consist of the following:

(1) PREWRITING

Analyzing the audience, setting the purpose, and brainstorming. The prewriting steps are listed for the students on the reproducible planning pages within each chapter.

(2) DRAFTING

Writing a meaningful message. First-grade students will begin writing sentences and build up to writing coherent paragraphs. (Keep in mind some students will begin with illustrations and labels.)

(3) REVISING/EDITING

Making sure the writing conveys its intended meaning. This step includes conferring with the teacher.

(4) SHARING

Reading aloud or publishing the writing for peers, teachers, parents, or another audience.

This section discusses each of these steps in depth and demonstrates how the weekly writing instruction fits into the writing process framework.

1 PREWRITING

Prewriting helps writers generate and focus ideas. Each of our lessons breaks down prewriting into three parts, described below.

Analyzing the Audience

The audience is *whom* the writer is writing for, the readers. It could include teachers, classmates, the principal, another class, or family members. Before writing, students should think about these people and put themselves in their shoes. Has the audience ever experienced what the writer is writing about? Audience awareness can be difficult for first graders because they generally assume the audience knows every person, place, and thing that they know. For example, if students are writing about a family picnic they can be less specific when mentioning the details if the audience is their family. However, if the audience is you, the teacher, they will need to be more specific because you did not go on the picnic with them and experience the things that they are writing about.

Setting the Purpose

The purpose, or main idea, controls the piece of writing. It is the message the writer wants to convey to the audience, or what the reader will ideally remember after reading the piece. The purpose is defined at the beginning of the writing to give the audience a map for the piece, and again at the conclusion to ensure the audience remembers the message. Emphasize for students that everything we do—beginning with waking up, eating breakfast, brushing our teeth, and packing our backpacks—has a purpose, and writing is no different. When we write, our purpose is often to share knowledge, to convey information, or to entertain. The purpose statement is scripted on the student planning pages to support students.

Brainstorming

Brainstorming means "storming," or searching the writer's brain, for ideas to support the purpose. This step helps students generate the main ingredients for the piece. To help focus the students on their purpose, allow them the opportunity to do a two-minute chat with a partner. First, young writers should color a picture to illustrate their main idea. Next, put students into groups of two and time them as they each talk for two minutes about their illustration. This will help streamline their thoughts before they begin to draft. Partners should be encouraged to ask questions if anything is unclear or confusing.

START:

S **Show** colors, textures, tastes, and smells.

T **Totally** describe people, places, feelings, and emotions.

A **Audience awareness:** Does my audience understand my ideas?

R **Reasons:** Are there at least three "ideas" or "reasons" to explain my purpose?

T **Tell** specific details, such as numbers (size, dates, ages, time) and seasons.

TIP

Make a list of two-minute chat partners and display it in the classroom. Keep groups consistent, so students feel comfortable with their partner. Rearrange only as necessary (i.e., to control behavior, encourage discussion, and so on).

Immediately following the two-minute chat, students should go back to their planning pages and write supportive words or phrases (for the purpose) in the brainstorming section of their planning page. ("Ideas" will be used with the narrative and expository prompts, and "reasons" will be used with the persuasive prompts.) Encourage students to come up with three ideas or reasons. They need only write single words or short phrases, as opposed to complete sentences, at this brainstorming stage.

Students can then apply the START acronym to their initial brainstorm and add adjectives to the ideas or reasons on their planning pages. Teachers of younger writers will need to read this acronym to them and give examples of how to expand brainstorm ideas. Make a poster-size copy of START (Appendix D, page 157) and hang it where students will be able to see it. With lots of repetition, examples, and practice, young writers will automatically include these important elements into their writing.

 DRAFTING

Drafting is when students begin to write about their idea in sentences and paragraphs. Using the planning page as a map, or guide, students will begin to draft their piece. Use any loose-leaf or lined printing paper that your students are comfortable with for this step. Following are more specific drafting steps for the different levels of writing. In terms of skill progression, first-grade students will begin writing sentences and build up to writing a coherent paragraph. Below you will find explanations of both sentence and paragraph drafting.

Sentence Drafting

Most first graders will be drafting sentences from September to December. The first sentence that the students will write is their purpose statement. They will then use their brainstorm ideas or reasons to draft more sentences to further enhance or explain their purpose. Although these sentences may naturally flow together like a paragraph, be careful not to call the writing a paragraph at this point. Later, you will explain that a paragraph is a group of sentences about the same topic, and students will move into paragraph writing, but for now, being asked to indent and to avoid irrelevant ideas will only confuse them. It is at this stage that we, as teachers, need to instill confidence and enthusiasm in writers and not bog them down with too much terminology. It is only when students feel comfortable with writing sentences that we can move on to the next step, drafting paragraphs.

Paragraph Drafting

Most first graders will begin to draft paragraphs in January. The purpose statement is written as the first sentence of the paragraph. Supporting sentences are then formed from the three brainstorm ideas or reasons in order to develop the idea and ensure reader comprehension. Encourage writers to use their words to "paint a picture" in the readers' minds. The last sentence of the paragraph, referred to as the closing sentence, should end, or close, the paragraph. It should be powerful and it should restate the purpose.

Until all students grasp the concept of purpose statements and supporting details, put sample paragraphs (student samples or teacher-generated examples) on the overhead or chalkboard and insert a sentence that does not support the purpose. Writers will enjoy locating this irrelevant sentence, and they will be more conscientious about choosing only relevant sentences in their own paragraph writing.

REVISING/EDITING

For first graders, revising is most successful when directed by the teacher, who can help with stylistic and grammatical elements, as well as fine-tuning using the acronym STOP (see right).

Carlos played on a baseball team this summer. The name of his team was the Tampa Bay Devil Rays. He played first base and catcher. Carlos hit five home runs for his team. <u>He also likes soccer.</u> His team won the championship and Carlos got a big trophy. Carlos loved playing baseball this summer!

Sample paragraph with an irrelevant detail

STOP:

S **Spelling:** Did I spell the words as best I can by sounding them out and using word banks and word walls? Did I use the dictionary?

T **Tells the purpose:** Does my first sentence communicate the purpose of my writing?

O **Organization and Out loud:** How does my paragraph sound when I read it aloud? Are there any parts that do not make sense, do not flow, or just sound funny? If so, could this be a grammar or punctuation error?

P **Punctuation and capitalization:** Did I use proper punctuation and capitalization?

Students can use STOP as a self-editing tool. Minor changes should be erased and corrected. If a lot of revisions are made, students should be encouraged to rewrite the paragraph. Use your discretion here. It is very difficult for students to rewrite everything, due to their developing fine-motor skills. We don't want to overburden them by having them rewrite every paragraph, but emphasizing neatness early on is essential to future performance. If you have computers available in your classroom, allow students the opportunity to computer-publish their final work from time to time.

 ## SHARING

Sharing is when writers read aloud or give their work to the intended audience. It gives the writing assignment a purpose and makes the process meaningful. In book three of the series, we discuss how to help students give and accept feedback while sharing during the editing phase of their work. In first grade, however, we emphasize sharing of the finished product.

Students should always be allowed to share their finished work in some way. Some teachers have a special "Author" chair that is painted or decorated with the title "Author." This chair is only used when a young "author" is presenting his or her work. Students cannot wait to sit in the chair and reap the benefits of their hard work, entertaining, informing, or persuading the audience with their written masterpiece.

Even without a specific chair, whole-group sharing should be done whenever time allows. Young students benefit from the insight of their peers as they strive to develop their own personal style. Whole-group sharing also gives students a sense of real accomplishment. Occasionally, you will come upon a child who is too shy to read to the class. He or she can choose a friend or the teacher to read the work to the class. Chances are this student still desires the recognition, but is just not yet comfortable reading in front of the whole group.

Allow the student author to call on three peers with questions or comments after sharing his or her piece. As the teacher, model appropriate comments or questions and guide students to focus on the grammatical and stylistic elements that you want to work on. You can compliment specific strengths—for example, "I really liked how you described your juice as 'cool and refreshing'." You can also ask questions that encourage students to include specific details, such as "Did you mean that you went swimming in a pool or at the beach?"

Do not try to share all of the pieces in one sitting, but rather, a few at a time. Transition times or snack time is a good time to share some pieces.

CONFERRING

Conferring can take place during any stage of the writing process to help students get "unstuck." It is very helpful to confer after students have completed a draft, and we recommend conferring with students at this time. Students benefit immeasurably from one-on-one teaching; conferring is essential to any writing curriculum.

Create a comfortable area to hold conferences. Some teachers like to conference at their desks; however, others choose not to use this area because it is too stimulating. Find a quiet spot in your room where the students will not be distracted, such as the back of the room, or an area sectioned off by a bookshelf or easel. You will need a table and chairs as well.

Invite students to read their piece aloud. When they finish, first provide positive feedback on the effort, praising progress made, word choice, use of a new convention, and so on. This will help build students' confidence. You may then offer one or two specific suggestions for revision.

Use this time to reinforce skills such as punctuation, capitalization, specific detail, or other topics that have been taught through the weekly mini-lessons. You can also use this time to address individual concerns with writing, or make suggestions to enrich or modify the writing for each student. Be sure students leave the conference with a specific idea about what to do next.

After the students are more comfortable, conferences can be more informal with the teacher just walking around the room and looking over each student's shoulder to observe his or her writing. This is also valuable to help students who may be getting off to a rough start.

Be sure to read the conferring tips in each lesson.

TIP

Create a writing center in your room. Use cardboard shelving units to store paper, pencils, erasers, a dictionary, and a thesaurus. If possible, set up this center near a computer, so that the students can utilize the computer during the writing process. Set up a few chairs so that children can work together during free time and so you can hold conferences with individuals and small groups.

Reward students periodically with a chance to share their work with the kindergartners, other first-grade rooms, or perhaps even the principal.

One way to manage sharing when the finished products become lengthier is to collect one piece from each student at the end of the month. The student can select the piece that he or she would like to share. These works can be placed in a decorated "Author" box and, whenever time allows, one or two can be presented.

Assessment

The biggest task in creating a class of first-grade writers is to get them writing. All learning, including writing, involves taking risks. Many first graders arrive reluctant to take these risks. A supportive, nurturing classroom environment will help these students begin to feel comfortable putting their thoughts into written words. With this in mind, we encourage you to examine your class, as well as your school or district grading policies, and proceed with an assessment plan that will work for you and your students.

Since the goal is to help students become confident, competent writers, we discourage the use of the red pen. Seeing their hard work marked up in red is disheartening and will not motivate young writers to take risks. Your mini-lessons, modeling, and individualized teaching during conferences are times to instruct and correct. Save the pen for supportive comments and gentle suggestions that will spur students to want to write again.

Many first-grade teachers set the goal of getting students comfortable with the writing process prior to winter break. Then, after the break, when most students are writing comfortably, they begin to formally assess.

Although assessment is vital to teaching writing, not everything that students write needs to be assessed—and not every error has to be corrected. Neither students nor teachers need to become overwhelmed during this learning process. There are several options for assessing final products. Four of the most useful ones are described here.

Focus on one problem at a time. Identify a recurring error—such as capitalization, punctuation, or incomplete sentences—then teach it in a mini-lesson, and show students how to edit for it. Allow time to practice. Then tell students that you will be checking their current work for that one error.

Assess select examples. Don't assess every single journal entry or writing assignment; instead, ask students to choose one piece that represents their best work.

Encourage self-assessment. Give students a copy of the writing checklists (see page 33 and Appendices E and F, pages 158 and 159) and have them assess themselves on specific criteria by checking "yes" or "no." Then quickly review their assessment. If your school uses letter grades, you can correlate the results of the checklist to a letter grade. You'll find copies of both checklists in the appendix.

TIP

Words from the high-frequency chart as well as the word wall can be copied into the personal word dictionaries (see page 34 for a description).

Collect writing samples in student assessment portfolios. Periodic writing samples—either originals or photocopies—can be placed in the student writing folders. (Our program advocates using student writing folders/portfolios to collect all student writing, including planning pages, throughout the year. In addition, a student assessment portfolio may be used to collect examples of work from all curricular areas.) The portfolio is a great way to show a student's growth over time. During a conference with parents, teachers, or administrators, these samples can highlight areas of growth, as well as areas of difficulty. Many schools set up assessment portfolios that begin in first grade and travel with students throughout the grades. The contents of these portfolios can also prove instrumental in detecting learning difficulties in young children.

> **Student Page**
>
> Name: _____ Date: _____
>
> **Writing Checklist: Paragraphs**
>
> yes no — Do I have 5 sentences?
>
> yes no — Did I begin with my purp
>
> yes no — Did I add detail by ma out of my key words?
>
> yes no — Did I use proper pu capitalization in my
>
> Appendix F

> **Student Page**
>
> Name: _____ Date: _____
>
> **Writing Checklist: Sentences**
>
> yes no — Did I begin with my purpose statement?
>
> yes no — Did I add detail by making sentences out of my key words?
>
> yes no — Did I use proper punctuation and capitalization in my sentences?
>
> yes no — Does my writing make sense?
>
> 158 — Appendix E

If your school does not have letter grades, you might make each of the above categories worth 5 points, for a total of 30 points. If you do use letter grades, you can calculate percentages to determine the letter grade.

There are many ways to assess writing in young children, and it's a vital task: assessment identifies areas of strength and weakness in students and helps you focus your instruction on their specific needs. You may find that your school or district requires you to follow a certain assessment plan, or that you are free to use your own. Whichever the case, find a plan that works for you and your students.

Meeting the Needs of Various Writers

There is no greater range in writing abilities than in a first-grade classroom, and, consequently, you will need to make accommodations for your students. All students develop at different rates, and the lessons in this book will be easy for some and challenging for others. However, the consistent format and use of the writing process throughout this program will facilitate comfort and ease with writing, as will the one-to-one weekly conferring between teacher and student. Conferences are tailored to individual writers' strengths and weaknesses. For your guidance, conferring tips will accompany each writing prompt. Be assured, however, that the writing abilities of all students will grow tremendously throughout the year.

How to Help Students Struggling With Word Formation

Be sure to let the students know that, unlike on a spelling test, during writing they will be allowed to use "invented" or "first-grade spelling" to spell words the way they sound. Begin a list of high-frequency words for writers to use.

Display the list so that it is visible in the classroom, and add a few new words each week. These words, which will be used throughout the year, will be referred to as the word wall.

Also, use a word bank to display words that are pertinent to the lesson. The word bank is a collection of words that students will want to use when writing a specific assignment. For example, after introducing and discussing the lesson, ask your students if there are any words that they think they might need to know how to spell. If so, list them clearly on chart paper or on the chalkboard. Students should be encouraged to use this word bank when drafting. Discuss with the students whether they think any words from the word bank should be added to the high-frequency list on the word wall.

Allow students to keep a personal word dictionary (see sample above). Here they can write the conventional spelling of words that they can't (or won't) use invented spelling for. To make a personal word dictionary in a spiral notebook, students will write the letter A on the top of the first page, and proceed all the way to the letter Z, so that it is alphabetized like a dictionary. For example, if a student asks you to spell the word *Florida*, you can write it on a small sticky note and have the student copy it into his or her personal word dictionary. This way you will not disturb the thought process of other writers by spelling words all day.

How to Help Students Struggling With Generating Ideas

An integral component of this writing program is brainstorming. Brainstorming helps students generate and organize ideas prior to writing. At the beginning of each writing assignment, you and the students will brainstorm together in order to create a list of ideas that can be used when writing. Be sure to clearly display the whole-group brainstorm so that it is visible to all students.

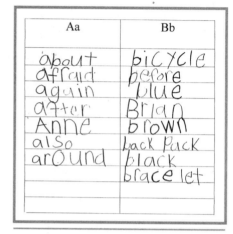

Aa	Bb
about	bicycle
afraid	before
again	blue
after	Brian
Anne	brown
also	back pack
around	black
	bracelet

Sample personal dictionary page

Encourage students to draw pictures next to the words in their personal word dictionaries so that the words can be more easily deciphered in the future.

Students will have more opportunities to generate and enhance ideas through the two-minute chat. During this time, students will meet with a peer to discuss their thoughts prior to drafting. Students struggling with generating ideas might need more than two minutes to talk with their partner about their illustration during the brainstorm phase (two-minute chat). You should also pair these students with higher-achieving writers who will be able to ask questions that generate more thought. For example: "You said that you like school, but what do you like about it? Is it something about our teacher or classmates, or is it a special project that you like best?" Students will learn to initiate these questions as the year goes on, through practice and much teacher modeling.

As you model, use a struggling student's brainstorming ideas. That way, he or she will be able to communicate the ideas with teacher assistance, while you are modeling for the whole class.

How to Help the Student Struggling With Fine Motor Skills

When young writers struggle with fine motor skills, a way to ensure that this does not interfere with the process of generating and organizing ideas is to take dictation from the student. You can take dictation yourself, or enlist the help of parent volunteers.

Another way to address students struggling with fine motor skills is by allowing them to use a classroom computer or a laptop, if one is available. These students can brainstorm and then go to the computer to draft their pieces. Here they will be less inhibited by the laborious task of forming each letter, and they can concentrate on getting their thoughts out.

How to Help the Struggling Writer Draft a Paragraph

By January, you will find that most of your students have had ample practice writing sentences. The focus then turns to paragraph writing. The emphasis will also shift to written, as opposed to pictorial, brainstorming. It will be necessary for you to model the new kinds of writing for your students.

Most of your class will be ready to move on to paragraph writing, but you'll also find a handful of students who appear far from ready. Rest assured that no matter how you accommodate these students, they are still gaining a lot by watching you model paragraphs. Certain students may require one-on-one conferring, in which you walk them through the assignment. Others may find success in a one-to-three (teacher to students) conference to ensure that they are on the right track.

Be prepared to differentiate or alter your expectations for students who are having learning difficulties. The "very young" writer should be allowed to

TIP

Depending upon the reading levels of your students, you may need to draw simple picture clues next to each idea on the whole-group brainstorm, so that all students will be able to find what they are looking for when they do their own brainstorming.

continue illustrating during the brainstorm phase and writing sentences during the drafting phase. Again, he or she will still be gaining a lot of ground watching you model paragraph writing.

Other beginning writers can be expected to develop a purpose statement; support it with one, as opposed to three, sentences; and end with a concluding sentence. When their fine motor skills and/or thought processes further develop, you can begin to expect three supporting sentences.

Use any accommodations that previously worked with these students: word walls, personal word dictionaries, extended two-minute chats, modeling, teacher conferencing, dictation, and laptop usage.

How to Help Early Finishers

Many writers, most likely the more able ones, will finish early. These writers can publish their writing on the computer, illustrate their work, or turn the writing into a book (complete with illustrations). They can also journal, reread past work, assist peers who are still working, write a creative story, or read for pleasure.

If a student is consistently finishing early, you may need to assess the reason. Is he or she ready to be taught to add more detail and support to his or her ideas? Do you need to ask for more sentences from this student? These are things that you can work on during conferencing.

How to Help Late Finishers

Some students, including those who require little or no accommodations, may consistently finish late. If you do not feel that these students need the sentence requirements modified, try to pace them throughout the assignment by giving verbal reminders that they should be moving on.

We wish you luck as you embark on your journey of teaching writing to first graders. Your enthusiasm for the process will motivate them. The instruction and practice you provide will give them the tools they need to express themselves on paper. By the end of the year, your students will be well on their way to writing proficiently.

Your job is an important one. You are laying the groundwork for what is to come. With this solid foundation, we will see many new generations of highly competent writers.

CHAPTER 3

September Writing Lessons

Daily Journal Prompts

How do you get ready for the school year?

To get ready for the school year, I _____ .

Imagine you are a feisty hornet. Describe your day.

As a feisty hornet, I begin my day by _____ .

Imagine you are playing soccer. Describe a good game.

A good soccer game is when _____ .

Imagine sitting around a bonfire and it is your turn to tell the story. Describe your story.

My bonfire story would begin with _____ .

What would you like to be when you grow up. Why?

When I grow up, I'd like to be a _____

_____ .

It is fun to spend time with our families. Different families have different things that they enjoy doing together. Describe something that your family does together.

My family likes to _____ .

What is your favorite time of day? Why? How do you feel at that time?

My favorite time of day is _____

_____ .

Tell about something that you are good at. How did you become good at it? How do you feel about being good at it?

Something that I am good at is _____ .

_____ .

Tell about a time when you felt happy. When was it? Who was with you? What were you doing?

I felt happy when _____ .

Describe an exciting or interesting activity that you recently did. How did you feel during the event or activity?

One thing that I did recently was _____ .

Describe your best day. Be sure to use lots of words that will "paint a picture" of this great day. Tell how you felt on this day.

The best day of my life was _____ .

Describe your worst day. Be sure to use lots of words that will "paint a picture" of this horrible day. Tell how you felt on this day.

The worst day of my life was _____ .

What is your favorite food? Write about it using words that tell how it looks, feels, smells, and tastes.

My favorite food is _____ .

Write about a good or bad dream that you've had. Be sure to tell how you felt about this dream.

A good/bad dream that I've had was about _____ .

Draw a picture of a robot that you might invent. Write about some of the things that it would do for you.

If I built a robot, it would be able to _____ .

Parents often tell us stories of things that we did when we were little. Describe something that you did when you were little.

When I was little, I _____ .

Every year in school we learn to do new things. Write about something that you hope to do this year. Why do you want to do this?

This year in school I want to _____ .

Help a new student identify your best friend in a crowd of people.
Draw a picture of your best friend and write sentences that describe how he/she looks.

Help me find my best friend. Here is how he/she looks: _____ .

Some people think that the weekends should be longer, and others think that they should stay the same. How do you feel and why?

I feel that the weekends should be the same/longer because

_____ .

Some children look forward to sleeping late on Saturdays, and others look forward to waking up early to attend special classes or go on special adventures with their family. Describe your typical Saturday.

On Saturdays I like to _____ .

As summer comes to an end, we look forward to cooler days and leaves changing colors. What is something that you like about fall and why?

One thing that I like about fall is _____ .

Sometimes we have relaxing weekends, and sometimes we have busy weekends. Describe one thing that you did over the weekend. Be sure to use details to "paint a picture" in the readers' minds and make them feel like they were there with you. Include feelings.

Last weekend I _____ .

What is your favorite animal? Use words to describe the sight, sound, smell, and feel of your favorite animal. Why is it your favorite?

My favorite animal is _____ .

Many families depend on cars to get them from place to place. What if there were no cars? Describe what your life would be like.

If there were no cars, _____ .

What is your favorite book? Does it teach you something, entertain you, or both? Describe this favorite book and tell how it teaches or entertains you. Why is it your favorite?

My favorite book is _____ .

Classroom Rules

GENRE: Expository sentences

SKILL: Capitalizing the beginning of sentences

STANDARD: Use correct grammar, spelling, punctuation, capitalization and structure.

ASSIGNMENT: Students will write about the importance of a particular rule in the classroom.

FOCUS: Discuss with your students the importance of rules in the classroom, at home, in our community, and in our world. What might our world be like if there were no rules?

MODEL: Ask students to offer some examples of rules that should be followed in your classroom. Record these examples on chart paper, the overhead, or the chalkboard. Be sure to make note of beginning capitalization as you write each example.

> William suggested that we should not run in the classroom because someone could fall and hit his head. That's a very important rule. I will need to start my sentence with a capital letter, So I'll make a capital "D" and write.
>
> Do not run in the classroom.

Model several sentences in this fashion, constantly reminding students that a sentence always begins with a capital letter. At the end of this lesson, ask a student volunteer to highlight or underline all of the beginning capital letters. If a student is struggling with this rule while writing, suggest that he or she use this highlighting technique on his or her draft. Go back and reread all of the examples as a group. Make sure that all students are watching so that they can make a visual connection to this capitalization rule.

PLANNING PAGE: Distribute the Classroom Rules Planning Page. Read and discuss the following steps: Analyzing the Audience, Setting the Purpose, Brainstorming, and Drafting. After each step, model and then pause to allow students to complete that step.

CONFERRING TIP

When a student has written a sentence or sentences and the spelling is not readable, ask the student to read to you and then write the correct spelling above the unreadable ones. Do not make students rewrite—the corrections are only put there so that the child can later reread his or her thoughts.

For a student who cannot write a sentence at all, use this conference time to write the sentence(s) that the student dictates to you based on his or her picture.

Name: _____

Classroom Rules

(1) **Analyzing the Audience:** The audience is your teacher and class-mates. Do they know the same things that you know about how the classroom should be set up and run?

(2) **Setting the Purpose:** It is important to/not to _____ in the classroom.

(3) **Brainstorming:** Draw a picture to show someone following a rule in your classroom.

(4) Write three ideas (key words) that explain your purpose.

_____   _____   _____

(5) **My Two-Minute Chat Partner Is:** _____

(6) **Drafting:** Using printing paper, copy your purpose sentence and write one or more supporting sentences using the ideas (key words) above.

A Summer Memory

GENRE: Narrative sentences

SKILL: Using ending punctuation: period

STANDARD: Use correct grammar, spelling, punctuation, capitalization, and structure.

ASSIGNMENT: Students will get to know each other by sharing summer memories.

FOCUS: Ask students to take a minute and think of all the exciting things they did over summer vacation. Which was their favorite? Also, reemphasize the significance of capitalization as a clue for the reader. Explain that we put a period at the end of a telling sentence to work like a stop sign, telling the reader that a complete thought is over. Read several sentences without pausing to illustrate the importance of ending punctuation.

MODEL: As students share their memories, record them on chart paper, the overhead, or the chalkboard. Be sure to make note of ending punctuation.

> Katelyn's favorite thing about summer was going to Disney World. I am finished writing my complete thought about Katelyn's favorite summer memory, and I am going to put a period, so that when we read it back we will remember to stop and take a breath before reading another sentence.

Model several sentences in this fashion, constantly reminding students that a telling sentence ends with a period. Also, reinforce the use of capital letters. At the end of this lesson, ask a student volunteer to trace each period with a red marker, or put a red star sticker over it. Go back and reread all of the examples as a group, making sure to exaggerate the "stop" at the end of the sentence. Make sure that all students are watching so that they can make a visual connection to this punctuation rule.

PLANNING PAGE: Distribute A Summer Memory Planning Page. Read and discuss the following steps: Analyzing the Audience, Setting the Purpose, Brainstorming, and Drafting. After each step, model and then pause to allow students to complete that step.

CONFERRING TIP

If a student is struggling with ending punctuation while writing, suggest that he or she place a red mark or sticker at the end of each sentence in his or her draft. Also, emphasize the importance of this rule in ensuring that the audience comprehends the student's writing.

A Summer Memory

Name: _____

(**1**) **Analyzing the Audience:** The audience is your teacher and class-mates. Did they experience the same special event?

(**2**) **Setting the Purpose:** Something special that I did over the summer was _____.

(**3**) **Brainstorming:** Draw a picture of the special event.

[blank box]

(**4**) Write three ideas (key words) that explain your purpose.

_____   _____   _____

(**5**) **My Two-Minute Chat Partner Is:** _____

(**6**) **Drafting:** Using printing paper, copy your purpose sentence and write one or more supporting sentences using the ideas from the ideas (key words) above.

Getting to Know You Part I

GENRE: Interrogatory sentences

SKILL: Using ending punctuation: question mark

STANDARD: Use correct grammar, spelling, punctuation, capitalization and structure.

ASSIGNMENT: Students will write questions to gather information about a classmate.

FOCUS: Tell students that in an interview we gather facts and information about a person by asking questions. Invite students to share some questions that they would like to ask a new friend while getting to know him or her.

MODEL: As students offer examples, record them on chart paper, the overhead, or the chalkboard. Be sure to make note of question marks at the end of each question.

> Connor would like to know if his partner has brothers and sisters. He can write the question . . .
>
> Do you have any brothers or sisters?
>
> We remember that sentences begin with capital letters. Questions, or asking sentences, end with a question mark. It is also like a stop sign at the end of the sentence, but it reminds us that a question has just been asked. Let's all try to read Connor's example.

Model several questions in this fashion, reminding students to put a question mark at the end of each question. At the same time, reinforce the use of capital letters at the beginning of the sentence. At the end of this lesson, ask a student volunteer to trace, with a marker, all of the question marks. Go back and reread all of the examples as a group, making sure to elevate your voice and exaggerate the question mark. Make sure that all of the students are watching so that they can see and internalize this rule.

PLANNING PAGE: Distribute the Getting to Know You (Part I) Planning Page. Read and discuss the following steps: Analyzing the Audience, Setting the Purpose, Brainstorming, and Drafting. After each step, model and then pause to allow students to complete that step.

CONFERRING TIP

If a student has a hard time using question marks, suggest that he or she highlight the end of each sentence to show that he or she has checked if the sentence asks a question.

Name: _____

Getting to Know You Part I

(1) **Analyzing the Audience:** The audience is your teacher and classmates. They want to learn some interesting things about their new class, too.

(2) **Setting the Purpose:** Here are some things that I want to learn about _____.

(3) **Brainstorming:** Draw a picture of your partner while you are thinking about some questions to ask him or her.

(4) Write three questions that you'd like to ask your partner.

1. _____

2. _____

3. _____

Getting to Know You Part II

GENRE: Descriptive sentences

SKILL: Writing answers to questions; presenting information

STANDARD: Apply acquired information, to communicate in a variety of formats. Speak effectively using appropriate language.

ASSIGNMENT: Students will record and present their interview data.

FOCUS: Students will now ask the questions they've prepared.

MODEL: Have students take out the planning page from last week and reread their questions. Tell students they can ask follow-up questions to get more details; give them an example, such as the following:

Question: Do you have brothers and sisters?

Answer: I have one brother and one sister.

Follow-up: How old are they? What are their names?

Answer: My brother is two; his name is Juan. Angela, my sister, is ten.

Sentence: Carlos has one two-year-old brother named Juan and one ten-year-old sister named Angela.

Then demonstrate how to record key words from the answers and turn them into sentences. You may want to have students practice by asking you questions and writing your answers. When students are ready, they can begin their interviews.

Once students have asked their questions and recorded their answers on the planning page, prepare them to present their information and introduce their partner. Discuss voice volume and speed. Give examples as you speak too loud, too soft, too fast, and too slow. Ask students to evaluate your examples. Finish by giving an example with a comfortable speed and volume.

Discuss the importance of making eye contact with the audience. This is a hard skill for young children, but the more it is reinforced, the easier it will become. If you have access to a video recorder, you may wish to videotape so the students can self-evaluate their presentations. If you plan on more student presentations throughout the year, make a checklist to evaluate clarity of information, speed, volume, and eye contact.

Allow each student the opportunity to introduce his or her partner to the class. Be sure to thank the interviewer for sharing with the class some important things about the interviewee.

CONFERRING TIP

If a student has a hard time writing the answers, you or the partner can record them.

Name: _____

Getting to Know You Part II

1 **Analyzing the Audience:** The audience is your teacher and classmates. Do they already know the things that you learned about your partner?

2 **Setting the Purpose:** Here are some things that I learned about my partner.

3 **Brainstorming:** Draw a picture to show what you learned about your new friend.

```
[                                                    ]
[                                                    ]
[                                                    ]
[                                                    ]
[                                                    ]
```

4 Write the answers to the questions that you asked your partner.

1. _____

2. _____

3. _____

5 **Drafting:** Using printing paper, copy your purpose sentence and write one or more supporting sentences using the ideas from the answers you wrote above.

Surprise Bag

GENRE: Descriptive sentences

SKILL: Using descriptive language

STANDARD: Present brief oral reports, using language and vocabulary appropriate to the message and audience.

ASSIGNMENT: Students will describe an object they've selected for show and tell.

FOCUS: A few days before the lesson, ask students to bring in an object for show and tell, something that will fit inside a brown lunch bag. Tell them it's a secret—they need to keep the object in the bag until the lesson is over.

MODEL: On the day of the lesson, hold up your own bag with an object inside. Describe the object with specific sensory details until students guess what it is.

Discuss how descriptive details helped students guess the item. Tell them that this week they'll get to write descriptive sentences about their show and tell object. Then they'll read their writing aloud to see if the class can guess what it is.

PLANNING PAGE: Distribute the Surprise Bag Planning Page. Read and discuss the following steps: Analyzing the Audience, Setting the Purpose, Brainstorming, and Drafting. After each step, model it and then pause to allow students to complete that step. When students are finished, have them read their sentences and invite the class to guess the object.

CONFERRING TIP

If necessary, help the student to develop clues by using START. See description of START on page 28.

Name: _____

Surprise Bag

(**1**) **Analyzing the Audience:** The audience is your teacher and classmates. They do not know what is inside your bag.

(**2**) **Setting the Purpose:** I have something special in my bag.

(**3**) **Brainstorming:** Draw a picture of the surprise in your bag.

```



```

(**4**) Write three clue words about your surprise.

_____   _____   _____

(**5**) **Drafting:** Using printing paper, copy your purpose sentence and write one or more supporting sentences using the ideas (clue words) above.

CHAPTER 4

October Writing Lessons

Daily Journal Prompts

We all look forward to going on field trips. If you could choose one field trip for your class, where would you go? What can you learn there?

I would like to take my class on a field trip to _____ .

Everyone gets angry sometimes. Tell about a time when you felt angry. What happened? What did you do? Would you do anything differently if it happened again?

I felt angry when _____ .

As we get older, we can do more things. We learn new things, such as how to ride a bicycle or read. We also earn special privileges, such as staying up later. Write about something that you can do now that you couldn't do when you were little.

Now that I am old enough, I can _____ .

There are so many things that we can do when we grow up. Think about some things that you would like to do when you grow up.

When I grow up, I'd like to _____ .

Do you have a favorite movie or TV show? What is it about? What is so special about it that makes it your favorite?

My favorite movie/TV show is _____ .

Being sick is not fun. Your parents take special care to help you rest and feel better when you're sick. What are some things that you can do if you have to stay home from school because you are sick?

When I am sick _____ .

We have five senses. They are sight, sound, smell, touch, and taste. Which do you think is the most important and why?

The most important of my five senses is _____ .

Taking care of a pet is a big job. Sometimes we have to ask a friend or relative to watch our pet while we go on vacation. What would you tell someone who is watching your pet? If you do not have a pet, you can pretend.

Here is what you will need to know to take care of my pet _____ .

Sometimes we feel embarrassed. It is not a very good feeling. Tell about a time that you felt embarrassed. What happened? What did you do? Would you do anything differently if the embarrassing situation happened again?

I was embarrassed when _____ .

Everyone can think of some good friends and some "not-so-good" friends. Think about one of your good friends. What makes this person a good friend?

A good friend is someone who _____ .

Describe how you would feel arriving in a new land. What is the first thing you would do?

If I were to arrive in a new land, I would _____ .

Being a parent is a lot of work. Write about one thing that you can do to help your parents at home.

I can help my parents by _____ .

Children enjoy playing at the playground. Write about the thing that you enjoy doing the most at the playground.

My favorite thing to do at the playground is _____ .

Parents are proud of their children when they do good things. Think about a time when you made your parents proud. Write about what you did and how you felt.

A time that I made my parents proud was when _____ .

Some people say that laughter is the best medicine. Laughing make us feel happy. Write about a time that you laughed so hard that your sides hurt.

I laughed so hard when _____ .

During the month of October, we begin to get excited about Halloween. Think about the costume that you would like to wear this year. Describe it, telling about the color and texture. If you don't know what you are going to be this year, write about something that you were in the past.

My Halloween costume _____ .

Some things that we do are easy. Other things that we do are hard. Write about the hardest thing you've ever done. What made it seem so hard? How long did it take you to do it? How did you feel when you were trying?

The hardest thing that I've ever done is _____ .

Families have different routines that they follow for different times of the day. Think about how your family spends their evenings. Write about your typical evening with your family. Try to think about what comes first, second, and third. Write your details in order.

On a typical evening in my home _____ .

What if television stations stopped broadcasting for one week. What would you do instead of watching television?

If I could not watch television for a week, I would _____ .

Invent a new toy. What would it look like? What would it do? Who would be interested in buying it?

If I were a toy inventor, I'd invent _____ .

Special Me

GENRE: Descriptive sentences

SKILL: Avoiding redundancy

STANDARD: Compose well-organized and coherent writing.

ASSIGNMENT: Students describe their special qualities.

FOCUS: Write the word *unique* on the chalkboard and explain that it means "one of a kind." Ask students to think of some things that set them apart from their classmates. Record their responses. Guide students to be specific; if someone says, "I am nice," ask them for examples, such as:

> Madelyn helps grandmas and grandpas at the nursing home.
>
> Robert reads to his younger sister and her friends.

Reread the examples with the class, pointing out proper capitalization and punctuation.

MODEL: Explain that this week students will write about how they are unique. Begin by sharing a few sentences about yourself. Be sure to write three to four sentences that all begin with the same word, such as:

> I can play the piano. I have been playing since I was five years old. I like to play Christmas songs. I play for my family and friends. I love playing the piano.

Read the sentences aloud and ask, "Did you notice anything that sounded strange? Did you hear a word I used too much? Listen as I read it again." Reread the sentences and help students notice the repetition of the first word, *I*. Say, "This can sound boring to readers. I'm going to rewrite my sentences so they all start with different words."

Demonstrate how you can rearrange the words in the sentences so that you do not change the meaning, but begin each sentence with a different word.

> I can play the piano. When I was just five years old, I began taking lessons. Christmas songs are my favorite to play. My family and friends listen to me play. Playing the piano is something that I love to do!

Tell students, "Now you will have a chance to write about yourself. Remember to start your sentences with different words!"

PLANNING PAGE: Distribute and discuss the Special Me Planning Page. After each step, model it, and then pause to allow students to complete that step.

CONFERRING TIP

Sometimes students have trouble recognizing why they are special. Some questions to elicit responses include:

What is one thing that you do very well?

What is something that is easy for you to do?

Name: _____

Special Me

(1) **Analyzing the Audience:** The audience is your teacher and classmates. They might not know all of the special qualities that you have.

(2) **Setting the Purpose:** Something special about me is that

_____.

(3) **Brainstorming:** Draw a picture to show something special about you.

```



```

(4) Write three ideas about your purpose statement.

_____   _____   _____

(5) **My Two-Minute Chat Partner Is:** _____

(6) **Drafting:** Using printing paper, copy your purpose sentence and write one or more supporting sentences using the ideas above.

The Best Game

GENRE: Persuasive sentences

SKILL: Persuading the audience

STANDARD: Communicate ideas in writing to accomplish a variety
of purposes.

ASSIGNMENT: Students persuade classmates to play a favorite game.

FOCUS: Ask the students to think of a television commercial that they like.
What does it want to sell? Tell them that advertisers use television and radio
commercials, billboards, and ads in magazines and newspapers to try to
convince us to think the way they do. This technique is called *persuasion*.

Tell students that they will write persuasive sentences to convince their
classmates and you to play a particular game. Remind students that they must
choose words carefully to capture the audience's attention, just as advertisers do
on commercials.

MODEL: To demonstrate effective word choice, share with the class samples of
prerecorded commercials or magazine ads. Make a list of the words that
appealed to students. Encourage students to use some of these words as they
write their sentences.

PLANNING PAGE: Distribute the Best Game Planning Page. Read and discuss the
following steps: Analyzing the Audience, Setting the Purpose, Brainstorming,
and Drafting. After each step, model it, and then pause to allow students to
complete that step.

CONFERRING TIP

Students may have
trouble thinking of
reasons to persuade you
that their game is the
best because they have
never thought otherwise.
To help them come up
with reasons, play the
devil's advocate and
argue that another game,
such as Candyland,
Chutes and Ladders, or
Trouble is better. This will
help students come up
with reasons why their
game is the best.

Name: _____

The Best Game

1 **Analyzing the Audience:** The audience is your teacher and classmates. Your favorite game might be unfamiliar to them or may not be their favorite game.

2 **Setting the Purpose:** The best game to play is _____.

3 **Brainstorming:** Draw a picture of your favorite game.

```
┌──────────────────────────────────────────────┐
│                                              │
│                                              │
│                                              │
│                                              │
│                                              │
│                                              │
│                                              │
└──────────────────────────────────────────────┘
```

4 Write three reasons for your purpose statement.

_____   _____   _____

5 **My Two-Minute Chat Partner Is:** _____

6 **Drafting:** Using printing paper, copy your purpose sentence and write one or more supporting sentences using the reasons above.

Halloween Costumes

GENRE: Descriptive sentences

SKILL: Using descriptive language

STANDARD: Compose well-organized and coherent writing
for specific purposes and audiences.

ASSIGNMENT: Students will use vivid description to create a picture of their
costumes with their words.

FOCUS: Share some descriptions of toys or clothes from catalogs. Ask if students can picture the items in their minds from the descriptions. What words helped them to create the picture? Explain that word choice is very important when describing something. Words that describe an object's shape, size, color, texture, and sound help readers create pictures in their minds. Tell students that they will be describing their favorite Halloween costumes.

MODEL: Generate a list of Halloween costumes with your students. Categorize them into groups (scary costumes, character costumes, funny costumes, and so on) on the chalkboard.

Ask students to think of their favorite costume. It may or may not be what they will be wearing this year. As students offer examples of their favorite costume, add them to the list in the appropriate category.

Then brainstorm a list of synonyms for the different categories. For instance, for *scary*, students might come up with *frightening, alarming, horrifying,* and *terrifying*. Show students how to describe something by comparing it to something else, such as *as black as night, glowing like a campfire,* or *as shiny as a new coin*. Encourage students to use synonyms and similes in addition to sensory words as they describe their costume.

PLANNING PAGE: Distribute the Halloween Costumes Planning Page. Read and discuss the following steps: Analyzing the Audience, Setting the Purpose, Brainstorming, and Drafting. After each step, model it, and then pause to allow students to complete that step.

CONFERRING TIP

To help students describe their costume with strong descriptors, use START (see page 28).

Name: _____

Halloween Costumes

(**1**) **Analyzing the Audience:** The audience is your teacher and classmates. They might never have seen your favorite costume.

(**2**) **Setting the Purpose:** My favorite Halloween costume is

_____ .

(**3**) **Brainstorming:** Draw a picture of your favorite costume.

[ ]

(**4**) Write three ideas about your purpose statement.

_____ _____ _____

(**5**) **My Two-Minute Chat Partner Is:** _____

(**6**) **Drafting:** Using printing paper, copy your purpose sentence and write one or more supporting sentences using the ideas above.

A Hobby of Mine

GENRE: Expository sentences

SKILL: Using time-order transitions

STANDARD: Use correct grammar, spelling, punctuation, capitalization, and structure.

ASSIGNMENT: Students will describe how they do a hobby using time-order transitions (*first, next, then,* and *last*). (See Appendix C, page 156, for a list of more time-order transitions for future writing.)

FOCUS: Share with students some of the hobbies that you enjoy. Encourage them to tell you some of their hobbies, and record them in a list. Tell them that this week they'll get to write about their favorite hobby.

MODEL: Distribute the A Hobby of Mine Planning Pages. Walk students through analyzing the audience and setting the purpose. Then ask them to draw a picture of themselves participating in their favorite hobby in the brainstorm box and to write three (or more) key words that tell about the steps required to do the hobby. Then have them do a two-minute chat with their partner. Next, model how to write the steps sequentially using time-order transitions as you draft (see the model paragraph at right). Finally, students will generate three (or more) complete sentences using their key words and the following time-order transitions: *first, next, then,* and *last*. Remind students that transitions are followed by a comma.

After students finish drafting, they will confer with you and revise and edit their work. On the last day, invite students to share.

CONFERRING TIP

If students are having a hard time using transitions at this point, introduce *first, next, then,* and *last*. These are easy ones to start with.

> My hobby is dancing. I go to dance class every Tuesday. First, I put on my dance clothes and shoes. Then, *my mom or dad drives me to the dance studio.* Last, I stretch *my legs to warm up my muscles and begin my lesson.*

Sample paragraph with time-order transitions

Name: _____

A Hobby of Mine

(**1**) **Analyzing the Audience:** The audience is your teacher and classmates. They may or may not have the same hobby.

(**2**) **Setting the Purpose:** My hobby is _____.

(**3**) **Brainstorming:** Draw a picture of yourself doing your hobby.

```



```

(**4**) Write down the things you need do in order to participate in your hobby. (If more room is needed, use the back.)

First, _____

Next, _____

Then, _____

Last, _____

(**5**) **My Two-Minute Chat Partner Is:** _____

(**6**) **Drafting:** Using printing paper, copy your purpose sentence and write the steps in order, using transition words. Remember to put a comma after each transition word.

Grade 1 Writing Curriculum: Week-by-Week Lessons Scholastic Teaching Resources

November Writing Lessons

Daily Journal Prompts

Describe an exciting or interesting activity that you recently experienced. Include how you felt during the event or activity.

One recent exciting event was _____ .

Write about the best vacation that you've ever had. Give specific details about what made it the best.

My best vacation was _____ .

Write about the worst vacation that you've ever had. Give specific details about what made it the worst.

My worst vacation was _____ .

Pretend that you are a dragon. Describe your life. Include details about your food and shelter.

If I were a dragon, my life would be _____ .

Imagine that you are hiking in the woods. You can hardly believe your eyes when you come across a treasure chest. What are you hoping to find in the treasure chest?

When I open the treasure chest, I hope I find _____ .

Many children like to play in sandboxes. Explain how to have fun in a sandbox.

To have fun in a sandbox, you must _____ .

VETERANS DAY   Our veterans have fought for our country so that we might have rights and privileges as United States citizens. Imagine that you lived in a place where you could not go to school. Describe what your life would be like.

If I did not have the right to go to school, _____ .

Describe your favorite playground. Give details about the equipment there.

My favorite playground is _____ .

Invent a piece of equipment that you would like to see at your favorite playground. What could children do with this new piece of equipment?

If I were to invent a piece of playground equipment, I'd invent _____

_____ .

Sometimes you need to convince, or persuade, people to do something for you. Convince your parents to take you to your favorite restaurant.

I'd like to go to eat at _____ .

THANKSGIVING Thanksgiving is a time when we think about all that we are thankful for. Describe one thing that you are thankful for.

One thing that I am thankful for is _____ .

Holidays are a time for traditions. A tradition is something that we do over and over again. Describe one tradition that your family keeps.

A tradition that my family keeps is _____ .

Chores are important in teaching us responsibility. Make a list of chores that you can do at home.

First, I can _____ .
Second, I can _____ .
Third, I can _____ .
Then, I can _____ .
Next, I can _____ .
Finally, I can _____ .

When you give instructions for something, you need to make sure your thoughts are organized so that the instructions can be understood by someone else. Give directions for brushing your teeth.

To brush your teeth, you must first _____ .

You want to go to a carnival, but your parents are not so sure that they want to take you. Choose words carefully and convince them to take you to the carnival.

I think that you should take me to the carnival because _____ .

Some children take swimming lessons and others do not. Convince all parents to ensure that their children take swimming lessons.

All children should take swimming lessons because _____ .

Write about a time when you felt scared. What was it that made you scared? What made you feel better?

I felt scared when _____ .

Write about a time when you felt sad. What was it that made you sad? How did you begin to feel happy again?

I felt sad when _____ .

There are many ways to get us from one place to another. If you were to take a trip and you had a choice to either fly on an airplane or ride the train, which would you choose and why?

If I were going on a trip, I'd like to _____ .

Lunchtime

GENRE: Lists

SKILL: Arranging items in order

STANDARD: Communicate ideas in writing to accomplish a variety of purposes.

ASSIGNMENT: Students will arrange items on a list in order of importance.

FOCUS: Ask students if they have ever made a list. Ask them what a list is and why someone would make one. Explain that a list is a series of items, names, numbers, and so on, often written in a particular order.

MODEL: Tell students that they are going to make a list for their parent(s) of all the foods that they like to eat for lunch. A list like this can help parents as they prepare lunches. Ask how they can arrange their lists (for example, foods that they like best first and foods that they like least last; sandwiches first, followed by drinks, fruits/veggies, and finally desserts; or foods listed in alphabetical order).

Explain that students can simply list their favorite lunch foods. They do not need to write in a complete sentence, using capitalization or punctuation.

PLANNING PAGE: Distribute the Lunchtime Planning Page. Read and discuss the following steps: Analyzing the Audience, Setting the Purpose, Brainstorming, and Drafting. After each step, model it, and then pause to allow students time to complete the step.

CONFERRING TIP

To enrich the more advanced writers, consider asking them to think of other lists that they can make and what purposes they would serve. Then have them follow through and make the lists (such as chores, school subjects, people on their block, class-mates, wish lists, and so on).

Name: _____

Lunchtime

(1) **Analyzing the Audience:** The audience is your parents. Your parents may or may not know the foods you like for lunch.

(2) **Setting the Purpose:** The following is a list of foods that I like in my lunch.

(3) **Brainstorming:** Draw a picture of your favorite lunch in the space below. Then, make a list of the foods that are in your picture. Arrange them in a way that is meaningful to you. Be sure that you can tell your partner how and why you arranged your list this way.

1. _____

2. _____

3. _____

4. _____

5. _____

(Continue list on the back if necessary.)

(4) **My Two-Minute Chat Partner Is:** _____

(5) **Drafting:** Using printing paper, make a final copy of your list.

Grade 1 Writing Curriculum: Week-by-Week Lessons Scholastic Teaching Resources

I Am Thankful

GENRE: Friendly letter

SKILL: Using correct capitalization and punctuation in greetings and closings

STANDARD: Communicate ideas in writing to accomplish a variety of purposes. Use correct grammar, spelling, punctuation, capitalization, and structure.

ASSIGNMENT: Students will express their gratitude through a friendly letter.

FOCUS: As you discuss the upcoming Thanksgiving holiday, remind students that they have a lot to be thankful for. This might be a good time to discuss *wants* versus *needs*. Tell students that they will be writing a letter of thanks to their parents or guardians. Remind them that parents and guardians know all of the special things their children have, but they may not know just how meaningful they are to the children.

MODEL: Make a class list of wants and needs. This is not always as easy as it seems because many six- and seven-year-olds think that if they really want something, then they need it.

Next, ask students to think about what they are most thankful to their parent(s) for. As students share their ideas, record them on chart paper, the overhead, or the chalkboard, being sure to model and emphasize proper capitalization and punctuation.

Then model writing your own thank-you letter. Discuss the important parts of a letter, as well as proper capitalization and punctuation rules for these parts. The *date* tells when the letter was written, the *greeting* addresses the recipient of the letter, the *body* is the message, and the *closing* ends the letter and states who it is from.

PLANNING PAGE: Distribute the I Am Thankful Planning Page. Read and discuss the following steps: Analyzing the Audience, Setting the Purpose, Brainstorming, and Drafting. After each step, model it, and then pause to allow students to complete that step. Next, pass out the letter template (Appendix A, page 154) and invite students to draft their letter. After students have completed their draft, distribute stationery.

CONFERRING TIP

If students are having trouble thinking about something concrete to be thankful for, have them think about something that they would not change.

I Am Thankful

(1) Analyzing the Audience: The audience is your parents/guardians. They have given you many things, but they might not know just how meaningful some of those things are to you.

(2) Setting the Purpose: I am thankful to you for

_____.

(3) Brainstorming: Draw a picture of something that you would like to thank your parents/guardians for.

```

```

(4) Write three reasons why you are thankful for this.

_____   _____   _____

(5) My Two-Minute Chat Partner Is: _____

(6) Drafting: Write on the letter template, and then transfer to a sheet of stationery.

Making a Turkey

GENRE: Expository sentences

SKILL: Writing directions

STANDARD: Write for a variety of purposes, including description, information, explanation, persuasion, and narration.

ASSIGNMENT: Students will write a turkey recipe.

FOCUS: One of the things that we associate with Thanksgiving is turkey. You can use the process of cooking a turkey to teach students how to write directions. Students will write their own version of a turkey recipe. Remember, a first grader's idea of how to cook the bird is very different from ours. The goal of this assignment is not to win the blue ribbon at the county fair cooking contest, but rather to think logically and sequentially. As many of these recipes turn out rather humorously, you might wish to copy them into a class "recipe book" to be shared with the cooks at home.

MODEL: First, review how to make a list. Ask students to volunteer suggested ingredients needed to make a turkey and make a list of them. (Be prepared for some unexpected ingredients!) This list will serve as a word bank when students write their recipes. Remind them that not all cooks use the same ingredients, so it is perfectly fine to choose the ones that they think are best.

Next, tell them that recipes are instructions for preparing and cooking food. A recipe must first list the ingredients, so that the cook knows exactly what and how much he or she needs. Recall that lists are written in a particular order and ingredients are usually listed in the order in which they are used. After the ingredients are listed, the directions are written in order. Point out that you can't stuff the turkey if you have already put it in the oven.

PLANNING PAGE: Distribute the Making a Turkey Planning Page. Have students prepare their list of ingredients to complete the purpose statement. Then have them draw a picture of themselves making a turkey on the back of the page. Next, have them write down key words to describe each step. They can talk with their two-minute chat partner to make sure the directions make sense; then they are ready to write their draft.

CONFERRING TIP

More advanced writers can be instructed to use time-order transitions such as *first, second, third,* and *last*.

Name: _____

Making a Turkey

(1) **Analyzing the Audience:** The audience is your teacher, classmates, and family. Be sure that you describe each step very carefully so that the audience will be able to follow your directions.

(2) **Setting the Purpose:** The things that you will need to cook a turkey are:

_____ _____ _____

_____ _____ _____

(3) **Brainstorming:** Draw a picture on the back of this sheet of yourself making a turkey. Write the steps that the audience should follow if they want to make a turkey. (Use the back if you need more room.)

1._____ 4._____

_____ _____

2._____ 5._____

_____ _____

3._____ 6._____

_____ _____

(4) **My Two-Minute Chat Partner Is:** _____

(5) **Drafting:** Write your recipe on printing paper.

Grade 1 Writing Curriculum: Week-by-Week Lessons Scholastic Teaching Resources

You'll Never Believe What Came Alive!

GENRE: Narrative sentences

SKILL: Sequencing events in a story

STANDARD: Use prewriting strategies to generate and organize ideas (e.g., focus on one topic; organize writing to include a beginning, middle, and end; use descriptive words when writing about people, places, things, events), and write for a variety of purposes.

ASSIGNMENT: Students will write a fictional story, containing a beginning, middle, and end, about a toy that came alive.

FOCUS: Ask if any students have seen or read *Toy Story*. After briefly discussing the premise of the story (the toys come alive when humans are not around; they talk, have feelings, and can move independently), ask if this story could be real. Discuss that fictional stories are make-believe. They could never happen in real life, but they are often written to entertain us. As a group, generate a list of fictional and nonfictional stories that the class is familiar with. Tell students that this week, they'll imagine that one of their toys came alive, and they'll write a fictional story describing what happens.

MODEL: Distribute the You'll Never Believe What Came Alive Planning Page and go over Analyzing the Audience and Setting the Purpose. Give students a few minutes to decide what toy to write about; you may want to have them talk it over in pairs or small groups. To model the next step—brainstorming what happens in the beginning, middle, and end—choose a familiar story or movie to illustrate the sequence of events. Divide chart paper, the chalkboard, or an overhead transparency into three sections. Write "Beginning," "Middle," and "End" at the top of each section. Ask students to summarize each part of the story, and write down on the chart what they say. As you write, reinforce the use of proper punctuation and capitalization. Keep the model on display as students brainstorm events for their own stories, drawing pictures and writing words.

Once students have finished their brainstorm, they can meet with their two-minute chat partner and then begin drafting. Consider modeling how to draft the story from your sample planning page to demonstrate the process. After conferring, revising, and editing, they can share their stories on the last day of the lesson.

CONFERRING TIP

If a student is struggling with putting his or her imagination into words, allow the child to role play while you record his or her ideas.

Name: _____

You'll Never Believe What Came Alive!

(1) **Analyzing the Audience:** The audience is your teacher and classmates. They may or may not be familiar with the toy.

(2) **Setting the Purpose:** I awoke in the middle of the night to find out that my _____ came alive!

(3) **Brainstorming:** Draw pictures to show what will happen in each part of your story. Then write words to tell about each part.

Beginning	Middle	End
_____	_____	_____
_____	_____	_____

(4) **My Two-Minute Chat Partner Is:** _____

(5) **Drafting:** Using printing paper, copy your purpose sentence and write what happened in the beginning, middle, and end of your story.

CHAPTER 6

December Writing Lessons

Daily Journal Prompts

There are lots of things that you can be when you grow up. Pretend that you are an astronaut. Describe what your life would be like.

If I were an astronaut _____ .

Describe what a good school day is like.

A good school day would be when _____ .

Describe a good school lunch menu.

A good lunch menu has _____ .

Persuade your friend to play your favorite game.

You should play _____ *with me because* _____ .

Many parents value their children learning a musical instrument. Do you think students should learn an instrument?

Students should/should not learn a musical instrument because _____ .

Think about your favorite fairy tale. Retell it using as many details as possible.

*I would like to tell you the tale of*_____.

Explain how to take good care of your teeth.

*To take good care of my teeth, I need to*_____.

Explain why it is important for you to help clean up at home or at school.

*It is important for me to clean up at home/school because*_____.

Write a detailed description of one exciting or interesting activity that you recently did. Include how you felt during the event or activity.

*One exciting thing that I did recently was*_____.

The different seasons bring about different kinds of fun. Think about some things that you can do only in the winter. What is your favorite winter activity?

*My favorite winter activity is*_____.

Winter holidays often include the giving and receiving of gifts. Think about a time when you gave something to someone. Describe the gift and how you felt after giving it.

*Once I gave*_____.

Playing in the snow is a popular winter activity. If you could build a snow fort, how would you do it? List all the steps necessary to build your snow creation.

Here is how I build a _____ .
First, I _____ .
Second, I _____ .
Next, I _____ .
Then, I _____ .
Finally, I _____ .

Write about one thing that you hope to do during your winter break from school. What are you imagining it will be like?

Over winter break I hope to _____ .

Everyone feels scared about different things. Think about a time when you felt scared. Describe that time in detail so that the audience would feel scared if they read your journal entry.

I felt scared when _____ .

Some children go to school year-round. These children have many small vacations throughout the year, instead of one big summer vacation. Convince your principal that your school should or should not be year-round.

Our school should/should not be year-round because _____ .

How to Build a Snowman

GENRE: Expository sentences

SKILL: Using time-order transitions

STANDARD: Write for a variety of purposes, including description, information, explanation, persuasion, and narration.

ASSIGNMENT: The students will practice sequencing as they write a "how-to" piece.

FOCUS: Children always look forward to the first snow of the year. One of the things that they enjoy doing is building snowmen. Ask students to recall a time when they built a snowman. If they have never built one, ask them to imagine how they would go about doing it.

MODEL: First, ask students to help you list some of the things that they would need (snow, charcoal, scarf, broom, branches, buttons, hat, carrot, and so on.) Record the list on chart paper, the chalkboard, or the overhead projector, and keep it up throughout the week to serve as a word bank for students.

Explain that often things must be done in order. When we write steps for a reader, we must make sure the order is clear. Ask students to read the time-order transitions on their planning page; discuss how these words would help a reader follow the steps of making a snowman. Next, ask them to think of the very first thing that they must do in order to build a snowman, and then to record it on their planning page. Have students continue to write the subsequent steps. Remind them that if their directions are clear enough, someone who has never made a snowman before should be able to follow the directions and successfully build a snowman.

PLANNING PAGE: Distribute the How to Build a Snowman Planning Page. Read and discuss the following steps: Analyzing the Audience, Setting the Purpose, Brainstorming, and Drafting. After each step, model it, and then pause to allow students time to complete the step.

CONFERRING TIP

Students may wish to act out building a snowman to help them put the steps in order. Stop them after each step, and have them write down what they just did.

Name: _____

How to Build a Snowman

(1) **Analyzing the Audience:** The audience is your teacher and classmates. Have they built a snowman before?

(2) **Setting the Purpose:** Here is how to build a snowman.

(3) **Brainstorming:** Draw a picture of yourself building a snowman.

(4) List the steps that the audience would need to follow if they wanted to build a snowman. Be sure to put the steps in the right order.

First, _____

Second, _____

Third, _____

Fourth, _____

And last, _____

(5) **My Two-Minute Chat Partner Is:** _____

(6) **Drafting:** Using printing paper, copy your purpose sentence, followed by the steps listed above.

Grade 1 Writing Curriculum: Week-by-Week Lessons Scholastic Teaching Resources

My Favorite Place

GENRE: Descriptive sentences

SKILL: Using sensory language

STANDARD: Use prewriting strategies to generate and organize ideas (e.g., focus on one topic; organize writing to include a beginning, middle, and end; use descriptive words when writing about people, places, things, and events).

ASSIGNMENT: Students will use sensory language to describe their favorite place.

FOCUS: We all have favorite places that we like to go to—for example, a restaurant, a store, a park, a friend's house, a relative's house, or a place in our own house. We have wonderful memories of these special places. Tell students that they will describe one of their special places in their writing this week.

MODEL: Ask students to think about their favorite place. Generate a list of favorite places so that you can model correct capitalization, punctuation, and spelling. This list can also serve as a word bank when the students are writing.

> Meghan's favorite place is Chuck E. Cheese.
>
> Tommy's favorite place is his grandparents' house.

Go back to the class list of favorite places. Ask each student to use sensory language, words that describe the sights, sounds, and smells of the place. They are then ready to begin their descriptive sentences.

> Meghan's favorite place is Chuck E. Cheese. The smell of hot Chuck E. Cheese pizza makes my mouth water as I walk in.
>
> Tommy's favorite place is his grandparents' house. My grandpa lies on the floor like a big kid and lets me climb on him as if he were a jungle gym.

Remind students that the reader should be able to hear, see, feel, taste, or smell what they are describing. Readers should also know how the writer feels about the place.

PLANNING PAGE: Distribute the My Favorite Place Planning Page. Read and discuss the following steps: Analyzing the Audience, Setting the Purpose, Brainstorming, and Drafting. After each step, model, and then pause to allow students time to complete the step.

CONFERRING TIP

If students are having trouble with this assignment, have them close their eyes and describe their special place to you or a partner.

Name: _____

My Favorite Place

(1) **Analyzing the Audience:** The audience is your teacher and classmates. They may not have been to your favorite place.

(2) **Setting the Purpose:** My favorite place is _____.

(3) **Brainstorming:** Draw a picture of yourself in your favorite place.

(4) Write three ideas (key words) that describe your favorite place.

_____   _____   _____

(5) **My Two-Minute Chat Partner Is:** _____

(6) **Drafting:** Using printing paper, copy your purpose sentence and write one or more supporting sentences using your ideas from above.

To Have or Not to Have . . . Cable T.V.

GENRE: Persuasive sentences

SKILL: Persuading the audience

STANDARD: Write for a variety of purposes, including persuasion.

ASSIGNMENT: Students will write persuasive sentences to convince their parents to either get cable or not to.

FOCUS: Discuss the meaning of cable and satellite television with your students. As a group, make a list of the pros and cons of having the service—number of channels, reliability of service, cost, and so on. Then ask students if they think having cable or satellite is a good idea. Tell them that this week they'll write persuasive sentences to convince their parents to either get cable or not to.

MODEL: Distribute the To Have or Not to Have . . . Cable T.V. planning page. Ask students to draw pictures/symbols showing what they like, or would like, to watch on T.V. and to write three key words that would help convince the reader why they need, or do not need, cable or satellite T.V. They will then do a two-minute chat with their partner before generating three complete sentences using these key words.

When students have finished planning, call them together and model writing sentences in favor of cable or satellite television, and then write a group of sentences in favor of regular television.

Finally, write a third group of sentences where the opinion wavers:

> I like regular television because we don't have to spend extra money for cable. If I had cable, I would like to watch Cartoon Network. Most of the shows I watch are on regular television.

Ask students if they can tell by your writing what side you are on. Discuss the importance of picking one side and sticking to it so that the writer knows exactly how they feel. Tell students to keep this in mind as they draft their sentences.

DRAFTING: After students write their sentences, ask them to reread their work and make sure the sentences all stick to the same idea all the way through; this will be the focus of most conferences as well. Students can share their writing on the last day of the lesson.

CONFERRING TIP

Students who have trouble sticking to one side of the argument may need guidance in deleting sentences that mention the flip side and replacing them with sentences that support their side of the argument.

Name: _____

To Have or Not to Have . . . Cable T.V.

(1) Analyzing the Audience: The audience is your parents. They may or may not have the same ideas about the importance of T.V. and the number of channels needed.

(2) Setting the Purpose: Our family should/should not have cable T.V. because _____.

(3) Brainstorming: Draw a picture of some things that you like, or would like, to watch on T.V.

(4) Write down three reasons why you would, or would not, like cable T.V.

_____

_____

_____

(5) My Two-Minute Chat Partner Is: _____

(6) Drafting: Using printing paper, copy your purpose sentence and write one or more supporting sentences that will convince your audience of your point of view.

Grade 1 Writing Curriculum: Week-by-Week Lessons Scholastic Teaching Resources

January Writing Lessons

Daily Journal Prompts

Every New Year, many people make resolutions to do something to better themselves. Some people make resolutions to eat healthier foods, to exercise more, to read more, or to be kinder to others. What resolution would you like to make to help you become a better person?

My New Year's resolution is to _____.

MARTIN LUTHER KING, JR., DAY We can learn important lessons from history. Think about something that you can do to help others live together in peace.

Something that I can do to help others get along is _____.

Write a detailed description of one exciting or interesting activity that you recently did. Include how you felt during the event or activity.

One exciting thing that I did recently was _____.

If you could have any wish come true, what would it be?

If I could have any wish come true, it would be _____.

What would you do or where would you go if you could make yourself invisible?

If I could make myself invisible, I would _____ .

Finish the following sentence with the first thought that comes to your mind. Then add details to explain your idea.

I like it when _____ .

Finish the following sentence with the first thought that comes to your mind. Then add details to explain your idea.

I don't like it when _____ .

We all lose things from time to time. Write about a day when you lost something. Be sure to include how you were feeling.

I'll never forget the day I lost _____ .

Describe one person you like to visit and tell why. Include how you feel when you visit this special person.

One person that I like to visit is _____ .

If you could go anywhere, where would you like to go? Why would you like to go there? What are some of the things that you imagine you'd do there?

If I could go anywhere, I'd like to go _____ .

Of all the animals that you know about, which is the best to keep as a pet? Why does this animal make a good pet?

I think the best kind of pet to have is _____ .

We all have things that we need to practice. Write about something that you need to practice. Be sure to include how you feel.

Something that I need to practice is _____ .

Explain how to have fun with Play-Doh or modeling clay.

To have fun with Play-Doh or modeling clay, you _____ .

Convince your teacher that you need to have more art projects in school.

I think that we should have more art projects because _____ .

Winter Vacation

GENRE:	Narrative paragraph
SKILL:	Writing paragraphs
STANDARD:	Communicate ideas in writing to accomplish a variety of purposes.
ASSIGNMENT:	Students will write a five-sentence paragraph about winter vacation.

FOCUS: Students now have had ample practice writing sentences for a variety of purposes. Although their work may have resembled paragraphs, we were careful not to call it a paragraph because the goal was to get all students writing sentences comfortably. Announce to students that as a result of all their hard work and practice, they are ready to take a big step as writers—they are ready to write paragraphs.

Explain that a paragraph is made up of a group of sentences about the same topic. Just as a sentence is made up of words, a paragraph is made up of a group of sentences supporting the purpose, or main idea. Tell them that the first sentence of a paragraph begins several spaces in on a line. It is indented to signal to the reader that a new paragraph is beginning. Show students examples from chapter books or magazine articles.

MODEL: Distribute the Winter Vacation Planning Page. Point out that the planning pages will now look different. There is no longer a space for pictorial brainstorming, but assure students that they can illustrate on the back or in the margins if they want to. In addition, there is a new section added for the development of an ending sentence, to bring closure to the paragraph. This can be written after the two-minute chat. Walk students through the steps of the planning page and model the actual writing of the paragraph. The best approach is to use an overhead projector and face the students as you write; then pause as they write, and continue on with this method until the planning page and five-sentence paragraph are complete.

Analyzing the Audience: Think aloud with the students about the most memorable part of winter vacation. Make the students aware that everyone has had different experiences. For example, some students may have traveled to visit relatives, while others may have had houseguests. Whatever the case, writers must provide vibrant details so the audience can feel as if they were there.

CONFERRING TIP

Although you are writing an example paragraph together, you may have to individually walk students through this same process as they write their own paragraphs. This may be necessary for the first few paragraph assignments. Students who need a little additional guidance may be able to conference in groups of three (one teacher to three students).

Setting the Purpose: Think aloud about several memories from winter vacation and model how you select one to write about. Allow students to talk with a partner about vacation memories for a few minutes so they can select a memory. Then call the class together, and using an overhead of the planning page, write the most memorable part of winter vacation—for example:

> *The most memorable part of my winter vacation was sledding.*

Pause and have the students fill in their purpose.

Brainstorming: List three ideas to support your purpose. For example:

> sled
> laughter
> hot cocoa/cookies

Pause and have the students list their three ideas.

Two-Minute Chat: On the next day, have students talk with their two-minute chat partners. This will help them generate details and examples before they begin writing. Chat partners should be encouraged to ask questions if anything is unclear or confusing.

Write in the **Ending Sentence**: This sentence restates the purpose with emotion or an overall feeling and/or prediction about the event. In your example, it could be as follows:

> *I cannot wait for the weekend so I can sled again.*

Notice that here you express your delight with sledding and your prediction that you will do it again.

Pause and allow the students to fill in their ending sentence. They can use your words: For example, *I can (or cannot) wait to . . . .*

Drafting: Following the two-minute chat and completion of the planning page, students are ready to begin writing, either the same day or the next. Display your planning page and model how you use it to compose a paragraph, flipping back and forth to the planning page so students can see exactly how it guides your writing.

When writing in front of students, do not hesitate to cross out, delete, or add ideas if they come to you. Tell students that this is what good writers do.

Stop after each group of words and ask students what to say in the next sentence. The final paragraph might look something like the sample at right.

Conferring/Revising/Editing: As students finish their drafts, meet with them for quick conferences, offering guidance as needed. On the last day of the lesson, invite students to share.

> *The most memorable part of my winter vacation was sledding. I loved my red sled because it was so quick, and it would spin at the bottom of the hill. This made my dad, my sister, and me laugh loudly. Afterwards, at grandmother's, we had hot cocoa with marshmallows and mint chocolate-covered Oreos. I can't wait for the weekend so I can sled again.*

Name: _____

Winter Vacation

① **Analyzing the Audience:** The audience is your teacher and class-mates. They may or may not have experienced the same event.

② **Setting the Purpose:** The most memorable part of my winter vacation was _____.

(sentence one in paragraph)

③ **Brainstorming:** List three ideas about your purpose.

1. _____

(sentence two in paragraph)

2. _____

(sentence three in paragraph)

3. _____

(sentence four in paragraph)

④ **My Two-Minute Chat Partner Is:** _____

⑤ **Ending Sentence:** _____

(sentence five in paragraph)

_____.

⑥ **Drafting:** Using printing paper, copy your purpose sentence and write supporting sentences using the ideas from above. Remember to indent your paragraph.

Grade 1 Writing Curriculum: Week-by-Week Lessons Scholastic Teaching Resources

My Good Friend

GENRE: Descriptive paragraph

SKILL: Using START to expand brainstorm ideas and write
              a paragraph

STANDARD: Use prewriting strategies to generate and organize ideas (e.g.,
              focus on one topic; organize writing to include a beginning,
              middle, and end; use descriptive words when writing about
              people, places, things, and events).

ASSIGNMENT: Students will write a paragraph about a good friend.

FOCUS: Prior to this assignment, make a poster or overhead of the START
acronym so that it is easily visible to the students (see page 28 for a
discussion of START).

Ask students to describe what makes a good friend so great. After a
few minutes of discussion, tell students that this week they'll get to write
a descriptive paragraph about one of their own friends. To help them
write a super paragraph, tell them you're going to give them a new
writing strategy called START, which they can use on any assignment to
make their writing stronger. Briefly go over the START poster or
overhead, mentioning that not all of the ideas in START will be used for
every writing assignment. For example, we would not describe the odor,
taste, or texture of our friend. (This will more than likely generate a bit
of laughter!) However, we would include hair color, eye color, and age
and/or birth date in our description. We would also include how we feel
when we are with this friend.

MODEL: It is critical to complete this assignment along with the students to
ensure a smooth transition to paragraphs. Begin by reviewing the process from
last week's assignment.

Analyzing the Audience: Make the students aware that not everyone knows
the same people. Ask them if their audience knows their friend. Tell them
that after reading their paragraph, the audience should feel as if they know
the student's friend.

Setting the Purpose: Fill in your purpose. For example:

 Michelle is my good friend.

Use **START** to
expand your ideas.

S Show colors, textures,
tastes, and smells.

T Totally describe people, places,
feelings, and emotions.

A Audience awareness: Does my
audience understand my ideas?

R Reasons: Are there at least three "ideas"
or "reasons" to explain my purpose?

T Tell specific details, such as numbers
(sizes, dates, ages, time) and seasons.

Pause and have the students fill in their purpose.

Brainstorming: List three ideas that describe your best friend. For example:

> caring
> supportive
> fun

Pause and have the students list their three ideas.

Two-Minute Chat: Have students talk with their partners.

Model: Show students how to use START to expand the brainstorm. For example:

> caring—always remembers birthday, sends a present, calls
>
> supportive—listens, talks, met in 6th grade
>
> fun—travel, shop, shows, fashion

Pause and have the students expand their ideas with START.

Ending Sentence: Remind students that this sentence expresses emotion and/or makes a prediction based on the purpose. It never introduces new ideas. For example, *I cannot wait to talk again with my friend, Michelle.*

Pause and have the students fill in their ending sentence. Again, allow them to use your ending sentence if they so desire: *I cannot wait to talk again with my friend, _____.*

Drafting: You may now compose the paragraph. The first sentence will be Setting the Purpose, followed by a sentence using each of the three expanded ideas, and then the fifth sentence, the ending sentence.

For example, the complete paragraph will be as follows:

> Michelle is my good friend. She is caring in that she always remembers my birthday with a phone call and a present. She also supports me by listening and giving advice any time I need to talk with her. No matter what, she is always cheering for me and encouraging me. And we have a lot of fun traveling and shopping together. I cannot wait to talk again with my friend, Michelle.

Tell students: "As a writer, I added more details that came to my mind while I was writing. Let students know this is okay, as long is it stays with the same subject or topic."

CONFERRING TIP

For struggling students, reduce the number of brainstorming reasons to two instead of three, until the students feel more comfortable composing. These students will then have four instead of five sentences for their body paragraph, which is perfectly acceptable.

My Good Friend

Name: _____

① **Analyzing the Audience:** The audience is your teachers and classmates. Do they know your friend?

② **Setting the Purpose:** _____
is my good friend.   (sentence one in paragraph)

③ **Brainstorming:** List three ideas about your purpose.

   1. _____

       (sentence two in paragraph)

   2. _____

       (sentence three in paragraph)

   3. _____

       (sentence four in paragraph)

Use **START** to expand your ideas.

S Show colors, textures, tastes, and smells.

T Totally describe people, places, feelings, and emotions.

A Audience awareness: Does my audience understand my ideas?

R Reasons: Are there at least three "ideas" or "reasons" to explain my purpose?

T Tell specific details, such as numbers (sizes, dates, ages, time) and seasons.

④ **My Two-Minute Chat Partner Is:**

_____

⑤ **Ending Sentence:** _____ .

           (sentence five in paragraph)

⑥ **Drafting:** Using printing paper, copy your purpose sentence and write supporting sentences using the ideas from above. Remember to indent your paragraph.

Thank You, Thank You!

GENRE: Thank-you letter

SKILL: Using parts of a letter—greeting, body, and closing

STANDARD: Communicate ideas in writing to accomplish a variety of purposes; use correct grammar, spelling, punctuation, capitalization, and structure.

ASSIGNMENT: Students will write a thank-you letter.

FOCUS: Ask students to think about all of the special gifts that they received during the holiday season. Which was their favorite, and who gave it to them? Tell students that this week they'll write a thank-you letter.

MODEL: Recall the friendly letters that were written at Thanksgiving time. Remind students that they should write the date on the top line in the right-hand corner. On the chalkboard, overhead, or chart paper, model proper capitalization and punctuation as you write a sample letter. Ask if anyone remembers what the first part of a letter is called (greeting). Remind students that the first letters of each word in the greeting are to be capitalized and that the greeting ends with a comma (e.g., Dear Grandma,). Your sample might read like this:

> Dear Grandma,
>
> Thank you so much for giving me the alarm clock CD player for Christmas. I put it on my nightstand next to my bed. The blue color matches my room . Before I go to bed each night, I set it for 7:00 a.m. Then I choose a CD to listen to and it helps me fall asleep. When the alarm rings in the morning, I know that it is time to get up and get ready for school. I love my alarm clock CD player!

Last, recall that the closing ends the letter and tells whom it is from. Students should sign their names right under the closing.

> Your grandson,
>
> Jaime

PLANNING PAGE: Distribute the Thank You, Thank You! Planning Page and go through it with students. Then hand out the letter-writing template (Appendix A, page 154) for students to draft on. Finally, hand out stationery for students

CONFERRING TIP

Some students may have to fill out the template with you (one to one). Be sure to have the students do the writing, to ensure ownership, attentiveness, and learning.

Name: _____

Thank You, Thank You

① **Analyzing the Audience:** The audience is someone who gave you a special gift. This person knows what the gift looks like, but may not know how much you appreciate it or what you like to do with it.

② **Setting the Purpose:** Thank you so much for giving me

_____.

③ **Brainstorming:** List three ideas about what makes this gift so special.

1. _____
   _____

2. _____
   _____

3. _____
   _____

Use **START** to expand your ideas.

S **Show** colors, textures, tastes, and smells.

T **Totally describe** people, places, feelings, and emotions.

A **Audience awareness:** Does my audience understand my ideas?

R **Reasons:** Are there at least three "ideas" or "reasons" to explain my purpose?

T **Tell** specific details, such as numbers (sizes, dates, ages, time) and seasons.

④ **My Two-Minute Chat Partner Is:**

_____

⑤ **Ending Sentence:** _____.

⑥ **Drafting:** Fill in the letter template and then transfer to a sheet of stationery.

CHAPTER 8

February Writing Lessons

Daily Journal Prompts

 **GROUNDHOG DAY** Will the groundhog see his shadow and allow us six more weeks of winter, or will he not see his shadow and award us an early spring? Which do you wish for and why?

I hope that the groundhog does/does not see its shadow because

_____ .

Most dogs do not like cats. Pretend that you have a dog who understands what you say. Convince the dog to allow you to bring home a cat.

I think that you would like a pet cat because _____ .

Cats are known to eat mice. Convince a cat to start a friendship with a mouse.

A mouse would be a good friend for you because _____ .

Think about all that you did yesterday. Describe the best part of yesterday.

The best part about yesterday was _____ .

 **LINCOLN'S BIRTHDAY** If you could go back in time, what would you ask President Abraham Lincoln?

I would like to ask President Abraham Lincoln _____ .

VALENTINE'S DAY Why do you need love? Think about all of the love you receive from family and friends. What would your life be like without that love?

I need love because _____ .

Sometimes when you ask for special things, your parents respond, "Maybe for your birthday." Think about one gift that you'd really like to receive for your birthday. Include how you'd feel if you received it.

I'd really like a/an _____
for my birthday because _____ .

Pretend you are a bear. Describe how you feel when it's time to hibernate for the winter.

When it's time to hibernate for the winter, I _____ .

Think about a time when someone told you a lie. How did you know it was a lie? How did you feel about this person not being truthful with you?

Someone told me a lie about _____ .

PRESIDENTS' DAY

The President has a lot of power and responsibility. Think about one thing that you would do if you were "President for the Day."

If I were "President for the Day," I would _____.

WASHINGTON'S BIRTHDAY

If you could go back in time and meet President George Washington, what would you ask him?

I would like to ask President George Washington _____.

BLACK HISTORY MONTH

It is unfair to treat people differently because of the color of their skin. What can you do to help treat people equally?

I could help treat people equally by _____.

Pretend that you are a waterfall. How do you feel? How do people, rocks, birds, and insects feel about you?

If I were a waterfall, _____.

Part of being a good friend is learning to take turns. Explain to a friend why it is important to take turns.

It is important to take turns because _____.

To grow strong and keep healthy, you need to eat a good balance of healthy foods. Describe two healthy foods that you eat. How do you feel about eating these foods?

Two healthy foods that I enjoy are _____ .

Unfortunately, it is often the unhealthy foods that taste good to children. Describe two unhealthy foods that you eat. How do you feel about eating these foods?

Two unhealthy foods that I enjoy are _____ .

What does the expression "You are what you eat" mean to you?

"You are what you eat" means _____ .

Describe the strangest food that you have ever eaten. Where did you eat this food? What was so strange about it? Would you eat it again if you had the chance?

The strangest food that I've ever eaten is _____ .

Imagine that your parents invited a dragon over for dinner. Describe the dinner.

When we had a dragon over for dinner, _____ .

99

Dear Visitor

GENRE: Formal letter

SKILL: Using parts of a letter—greeting, body, and closing

STANDARD: Write letters, reports, and stories based on acquired information. Compose well-organized and coherent writing for specific purposes and audiences.

ASSIGNMENT: Students will write a formal letter describing their school to a visitor.

FOCUS: Ask students to think about all of the things that make their school a special place. Tell them to pretend that a visitor is coming to their school. This visitor has never been to the school before.

MODEL: Ask students to brainstorm all of the special things that they would want the visitor to see. Record the list on the overhead, chart paper, or the chalkboard. Students can use this as a word bank. Include examples of formal language that they might include in their letters.

Before students begin their planning pages, remind them of the format of a letter (see page 70). Tell students that they should use colorful, descriptive words that will make the visitor want to come and see their suggested sights. Explain, for example, that the sentence *Please go see the auditorium* can be made more colorful by using a better choice of descriptive words: *You should visit our auditorium, with its soft, cushiony chairs and its huge, red velvet curtains.* Take a few minutes to allow student volunteers to share more examples of simple sentences that can be made more descriptive. Record a list of examples.

PLANNING PAGE: Distribute the Dear Visitor Planning Page and letter template (Appendix A, page 154). Read and discuss the following steps: Analyzing the Audience, Setting the Purpose, Brainstorming, and Drafting. After each step, model, and then pause to allow students to complete that step. Students can draft on the letter template and then write their final copy on stationery.

CONFERRING TIP

If students are not familiar with how their school compares and contrasts with others, share some of your experiences.

Dear Visitor

① **Analyzing the Audience:** The audience is a visitor who has never been to your school before. This person knows nothing about where things are and what special things go on in your class.

② **Setting the Purpose:** There are some special things that you should see while you are visiting _____ School.

(sentence one in letter)

③ **Brainstorming:** List three ideas about what you think the visitor would like to see.

1. _____
_____

(sentence two in letter)

2. _____
_____

(sentence three in letter)

3. _____
_____

(sentence four in letter)

Use **START** to expand your ideas.

S Show colors, textures, tastes, and smells.

T Totally describe people, places, feelings, and emotions.

A Audience awareness: Does my audience understand my ideas?

R Reasons: Are there at least three "ideas" or "reasons" to explain my purpose?

T Tell specific details, such as numbers (sizes, dates, ages, time) and seasons.

④ **My Two-Minute Chat Partner Is:** _____

⑤ **Ending Sentence:** _____.

(sentence five in letter)

⑥ **Drafting:** Fill in the letter template and then transfer to a sheet of stationery.

My Invention

GENRE: Expository paragraph

SKILL: Using elaboration

STANDARD: Demonstrate focus, organization, elaboration, and integration in
              written compositions.

ASSIGNMENT: Students will write an expository paragraph explaining
              something that they imagine themselves inventing.

FOCUS: Discuss inventors with students. Invite students to give examples of
important inventions. Ask how these inventions are important in our daily life.
(They often make our jobs easier or save us time.) Where do inventors get
ideas? What inventions would students like to see?

MODEL: Tell students that they'll be writing about an invention they would like
to create. Remind them that all the sentences in the paragraph must relate to
the purpose—all sentences will describe the invention and what it is used for.

Before students begin writing, take some time to review paragraph
drafting and the example exercise described on page 29. Put sample paragraphs
on the overhead, chalkboard, or chart paper. Insert one or two sentences that
do not belong with the topic sentence. Students will enjoy trying to locate
these sentences and crossing them out. While these sentences may be true or
important, if they do not support, or explain, the topic sentence, then they
do not belong in that paragraph. Adding this exercise to your daily morning
routine will prove beneficial in the long run.

PLANNING PAGE: Distribute the My Invention Planning Page. Read and
discuss the following steps: Analyzing the Audience, Setting the Purpose,
Brainstorming, and Drafting. After each step, model, and then pause to allow
students to complete that step.

CONFERRING TIP

Walk the students through START. Make suggestions and allow students to write them down.

My Invention

Name: _____

(1) **Analyzing the Audience:** The audience is your teacher and class-mates. They do not know about your invention.

(2) **Setting the Purpose:** Some day I would like to invent

_____.

(sentence one in paragraph)

(3) **Brainstorming:** List three ideas about your purpose.

> Use **START** to expand your ideas.
>
> **S** Show colors, textures, tastes, and smells.
>
> **T** Totally describe people, places, feelings, and emotions.
>
> **A** Audience awareness: Does my audience understand my ideas?
>
> **R** Reasons: Are there at least three "ideas" or "reasons" to explain my purpose?
>
> **T** Tell specific details, such as numbers (sizes, dates, ages, time) and seasons.

1. _____

_____

(sentence two in paragraph)

2. _____

_____

(sentence three in paragraph)

3. _____

_____

(sentence four in paragraph)

(4) **My Two-Minute Chat Partner Is:** _____

(5) **Ending Sentence:** _____.

(sentence five in paragraph)

(6) **Drafting:** Using printing paper, write your paragraph. First, copy your purpose sentence. Then, make a sentence out of each brainstorming idea. Finally, copy your ending sentence.

School Fun

GENRE: Narrative paragraph

SKILL: Writing paragraphs—purpose, supporting sentences, and sentences of elaboration

STANDARD: Communicate ideas in writing to accomplish a variety of purposes. Demonstrate focus, organization, and elaboration, in writing.

ASSIGNMENT: Students will use elaboration to describe their favorite thing about school in a narrative paragraph.

FOCUS: Ask students what they like best about school. After a few minutes of discussion, tell them that this week they'll write about their favorite school activity.

MODEL: As a teacher, you are continuously reviewing skills. You have taught a lot about paragraphs in a very short time. This lesson will be a good time to review what you've taught:

The purpose, or topic sentence, is the sentence that controls the paragraph. For example: *One of the things that I enjoy the most about school is _____.*

The supporting sentences, which are formed from the brainstorm ideas or reasons, add detail and help explain or support the purpose. For example:

> One of the things that I enjoy most about school is science. Mr. Evans lets us do fun experiments. We use special equipment that scientists use. Sometimes we make things that we can bring home. This year we learned about our five senses. We also learned about static electricity.

Remind students that START can help them elaborate. Some students will enjoy elaborating on every idea, while others may begin by elaborating on one or two. There is no rule that dictates which ideas should be elaborated upon.

PLANNING PAGE: Distribute the School Fun Planning Page. Read and discuss the following steps: Analyzing the Audience, Setting the Purpose, Brainstorming, and Drafting. After each step, model it, and then pause to allow students to complete that step.

CONFERRING TIP

Help students elaborate on ideas for which they show excitement or enthusiasm.

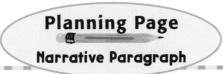
Name: _____

School Fun

(1) **Analyzing the Audience:** The audience is your teacher and classmates. They all enjoy different things about school.

(2) **Setting the Purpose:** One of the things that I enjoy most about school is _____.

(sentence one in paragraph)

(3) **Brainstorming:** List three ideas about your purpose.

1. _____

_____

(sentence two in paragraph)

2. _____

_____

(sentence three in paragraph)

3. _____

_____

(sentence four in paragraph)

Use **START** to expand your ideas.

S Show colors, textures, tastes, and smells.

T Totally describe people, places, feelings, and emotions.

A Audience awareness: Does my audience understand my ideas?

R Reasons: Are there at least three "ideas" or "reasons" to explain my purpose?

T Tell specific details, such as numbers (sizes, dates, ages, time) and seasons.

(4) **My Two-Minute Chat Partner Is:** _____

(5) **Ending Sentence:** _____.

(sentence five in paragraph)

(6) **Drafting:** Using printing paper, write your paragraph. First, copy your purpose sentence. Then, make a sentence out of each brainstorming idea. Finally, copy your ending sentence.

Grade 1 Writing Curriculum: Week-by-Week Lessons Scholastic Teaching Resources

Something I Do Well

GENRE: Narrative paragraph

SKILL: Writing compound sentences

STANDARD: Use correct grammar, spelling, and punctuation.

ASSIGNMENT: Students will write a paragraph describing something they do well.

FOCUS: Talk about something that you do well, and ask students to share things they do well. Record the list on the overhead, chart paper, or the chalkboard. Tell students that this week they'll write about one specific thing they do well.

MODEL: Distribute the Something I Do Well Planning Page and go over Analyzing the Audience and Setting the Purpose. Have students draw a picture of themselves performing the activity. Then ask them to think of three ideas that relate to this talent and write three key words under their pictures.

After students talk with their chat partner, call the class together and model how to write a compound sentence, the skill for the week. Tell them that a compound sentence is one sentence made up of two smaller sentences. To make writing sound interesting, writers should use a variety of sentences, some long and some short. Compound sentences are one way to write longer sentences. Generate a list of compound sentences with students, showing how a special kind of word called a *conjunction* can be used to hook the two sentences together. Explain that *conjunction* is just a name for a group of words that join words and sentences together; they are *and, but, or, nor, so,* and *yet*—all words that students know and use. Give them an example of a compound sentence, such as

> Tony plays competitive baseball on a team, and he plays for fun with his friends.

Ask students to identify the conjunction. Cover up the comma and the word *and.* Show students that they can tell a sentence is a compound sentence if each of the parts can stand alone as a sentence.

After generating and discussing several examples, tell students to include at least one compound sentence in their writing this week. Leave the examples and list of conjunctions displayed while students write. Remind them to put a comma before a conjunction that will join two sentences. After conferring, revising, and editing, they can share their stories on the last day of the lesson.

CONFERRING TIP

Find examples of compound sentences in classroom reading material. Draw attention to the comma and conjunction, and have students look for two smaller sentences that can stand independently.

Name: _____

Something I Do Well

① **Analyzing the Audience:** The audience is your teacher and classmates. They may or may not have the same talents as you.

② **Setting the Purpose:** Something that I do well is _____.

③ **Brainstorming:** Draw a picture of yourself doing something you feel you are good at.

④ Write down three ideas about your special talent.

_____   _____   _____

⑤ **My Two-Minute Chat Partner Is:** _____

⑥ **Drafting:** Using printing paper, copy your purpose sentence and write one or more supporting sentences using the ideas from above. Use a conjunction (*and, but, or, nor, so, yet*) to write at least one compound sentence.

CHAPTER 9

March Writing Lessons

Daily Journal Prompts

Describe the best birthday party that you've ever been to. What things made it "the best"?

The best birthday party I've been to was _____ .

Describe your favorite movie. Tell about the characters, setting, problem, and solution.

My favorite movie is _____ .

Describe a perfect tree house.

A perfect tree house would have _____ .

Describe a fun goody bag for a birthday party.

A fun goody bag will have _____

Describe a good activity for a rainy day.

A good rainy-day activity is _____ .

Write a detailed description of one exciting or interesting activity that you recently did. Include how you felt during the activity.

One exciting thing that I did recently was _____ .

Think about all of the desserts that you have ever eaten. Describe your favorite dessert. How does it look and taste?

My favorite dessert is _____ .

Think about all of the special places in your home. Which place is your favorite? What do you do in this special place? How do you feel when you are there?

My favorite place in my home is _____ .

Describe how you would like to have fun on a Saturday. What would you do? Who would you do it with?

Some Saturday, I'd like to _____ .

Finish the following sentence with the first thought that comes to your mind. Then add details to explain your statement.

I'd like to solve the problem of _____ .

Describe your adventures as a seedling. How do you travel? How will you eventually sprout?

If I were a seedling, _____ .

SPRING   Describe your life as a flower. What kind of flower are you? What do you look like? Where do you live? What do you need to survive?

If I were a flower, I'd like to be _____ .

Legend has it that you'll find your dream at the end of the rainbow. What would you like to find at the end of a rainbow?

I'd like to follow a rainbow and find _____ .

ST. PATRICK'S DAY   A symbol of good luck for the Irish is the shamrock. Describe something that you value as a symbol of good luck.

My symbol of good luck is _____ .

Think about some things that you like to do with your best friend. What do the two of you enjoy doing the most?

When I play with my best friend, we like to _____

While riding your bicycle it turns into a motorcycle. Describe your adventures.

When my bicycle became a motorcycle, _____ .

Describe losing a tooth.

When I lose a tooth, I feel _____

_____ .

Describe a train or boat ride.

A train/boat ride is like _____

_____ .

Think about something that you'd really like to do when you become a parent.

When I become a parent _____ .

Describe one person who is important to you. Why is this person so important to you? How do you feel when you are with him or her?

A very important person to me is _____ .

Dear Teacher

GENRE: Persuasive letter

SKILL: Writing supporting sentences

STANDARD: Write letters, reports, and stories based on acquired information.

ASSIGNMENT: Students will write a persuasive letter to their teacher.

FOCUS: Review with students the persuasive sentences that they wrote in the Week 7 Lesson. Remind them that in persuasive writing, their goal is to try to convince the reader to think the way they do. In October they tried to convince their teacher and classmates the best game to play. This week, they will begin to write a persuasive letter to their teacher about whether they should have homework on weekends or weekdays.

MODEL: Before filling out the planning pages, tell students that the hardest thing about good persuasive writing is choosing a position and then supporting it. Students do not want to become wishy-washy, fluctuating between both sides of the argument, listing the pros and cons of each. They need to pick one side only and be sure to support it with reasons. Before they begin their writing, they should know, without a doubt, which side they will argue. Practice this type of debate by bringing up the examples of recess versus no recess and/or year-round school versus traditional school.

Since this project involves writing a letter as opposed to a paragraph, it is a good opportunity to review the parts of a letter: date, greeting, body, and closing.

PLANNING PAGE: Distribute the Dear Teacher Planning Page and letter template (Appendix A, page 154). Read and discuss the following steps: Analyzing the Audience, Setting the Purpose, Brainstorming, and Drafting. After each step, model, and then pause to allow students to complete that step.

CONFERRING TIP

If students offer support for both sides of an issue, help them recognize this and eliminate the less heartfelt side of the argument.

Name: _____

Dear Teacher

(**1**) **Analyzing the Audience:** The audience is your teacher. He or she may or may not agree with your side of the argument. You'll need to choose words that really sound convincing.

(**2**) **Setting the Purpose:** I think that we should have homework on _____ only. (Choose weekends or weekdays.)
(sentence one in letter)

(**3**) **Brainstorming:** List three reasons to support your choice.

1. _____

_____
(sentence two in letter)

2. _____

_____
(sentence three in letter)

3. _____

_____
(sentence four in letter)

Use **START** to expand your ideas.

S **Show** colors, textures, tastes, and smells.

T **Totally describe** people, places, feelings, and emotions.

A **Audience awareness:** Does my audience understand my ideas?

R **Reasons:** Are there at least three "ideas" or "reasons" to explain my purpose?

T **Tell** specific details, such as numbers (sizes, dates, ages, time) and seasons.

(**4**) **My Two-Minute Chat Partner Is:** _____

(**5**) **Ending Sentence:** _____.
(sentence five in letter)

(**6**) **Drafting:** Fill in the letter template and then transfer to stationery.

My Favorite Toy

GENRE: Descriptive paragraph

SKILL: Using descriptive language (similes)

STANDARD: Communicate ideas in writing to accomplish a variety of purposes.

ASSIGNMENT: Students will write a descriptive paragraph that includes similes.

FOCUS: Ask students to think about their favorite toy. How would they describe it to someone who has never seen it? Remind them that the careful choice of words will help to paint a picture in the readers' minds.

MODEL: Next, recall the Week 15 Lesson, My Favorite Place. Students were asked to allow the reader to hear, see, feel, taste, or smell the place that was being described. Tell students that this week they will write a descriptive paragraph about their favorite toy. Not all of the five "sense" words will apply to their topic. For example, their favorite toy might not have a "taste." Students, however, should try to use as many of the senses as possible when describing their favorite toy. Ask, *How does your teddy bear look? How does it feel? How does it smell? Does it make any sounds?*

Introduce the use of similes. Define a simile as a comparison—using *like* or *as*—that compares two unlike things. Write some examples on the chalkboard, overhead, or chart paper, such as *The horse ran like the wind.* Ask students to describe what these words called up in their minds. Encourage students to use descriptive language and similes in this project to make their writing come alive.

PLANNING PAGE: Distribute the My Favorite Toy Planning Page. Read and discuss the following steps: Analyzing the Audience, Setting the Purpose, Brainstorming, and Drafting. After each step, model it, and then pause to allow students to complete that step.

CONFERRING TIP

Help students develop a specific simile by having them write a noun followed by the word *like* or *as*. Then have them generate a comparison object.

Name: _____

My Favorite Toy

(1) Analyzing the Audience: The audience is your teacher and class-mates. They may or may not be familiar with your favorite toy.

(2) Setting the Purpose: My favorite toy is_____.
(sentence one in paragraph)

(3) Brainstorming: List three words that describe that toy. Try to use words that appeal to the five senses—sight, sound, touch, taste, and smell.

1. _____

_____

(sentence two in paragraph)

2. _____

_____

(sentence three in paragraph)

3. _____

_____

(sentence four in paragraph)

> Use **START** to expand your ideas.
>
> **S** Show colors, textures, tastes, and smells.
>
> **T** Totally describe people, places, feelings, and emotions.
>
> **A** Audience awareness: Does my audience understand my ideas?
>
> **R** Reasons: Are there at least three "ideas" or "reasons" to explain my purpose?
>
> **T** Tell specific details, such as numbers (sizes, dates, ages, time) and seasons.

(4) My Two-Minute Chat Partner Is: _____

(5) Ending Sentence: _____.
(sentence five in paragraph)

(6) Drafting: Using printing paper, write your paragraph. First, copy your purpose sentence. Then, make a sentence out of each brain-storming idea. Finally, copy your ending sentence.

The Best Day of My Life

GENRE: Narrative paragraph

SKILL: Sequencing and using time-order transitions

STANDARD: Relate character, setting, and plot to real-life situations.

ASSIGNMENT: Students will write a personal narrative telling something about their life.

FOCUS: Ask students to think about the best day of their life. Be ready for a handful of students to say that they have so many it is hard to choose. To keep them focused, ask them to list the days and then choose one that they'd like to relive and write about today.

MODEL: Next, tell students that they are going to tell the story of this great day by writing a narrative paragraph. They will need to tell the story in order so that it makes sense. Give examples of sequence and time-order words that help readers understand when events take place.

> The best day of my life was my first trip to Rocky Point. When we walked through the gate, I couldn't believe all the rides! First, my sister and I ran to the ferris wheel so we could get a good view of the park.

PLANNING PAGE: On the first brainstorming line of The Best Day of My Life Planning Page, students will try to jot down a word or phrase that describes the beginning of this day. On the second line, they will try to think of what happened next, and so forth.

Before students begin their draft, share this short list of simple time-order transition words. Encourage students to use them to show the passing of time in their stories.

after	at the same time	meanwhile
at last	finally	when
from then on	later on	as
during	again	best of all
lastly	before	first of all
soon	first	last of all
afterward	then	next
immediately	in the meantime	while

CONFERRING TIP

Most students will write their stories in one continuous paragraph. This is fine, as you want to encourage, not inhibit, the development of the story. More advanced writers may wish to be shown when to begin new paragraphs. They can think of it like scenes from a movie. If it sounds like the beginning of a new "scene," such as a different time of day, then they should begin a new paragraph.

Name: _____

The Best Day of My Life

① **Analyzing the Audience:** The audience is your teacher and class-mates. They most likely did not experience this special day with you.

② **Setting the Purpose:** The best day of my life was when

_____.

(sentence one in paragraph)

③ **Brainstorming:** List three ideas about your special day. Be sure to list your ideas in the order in which they happened.

1. _____

_____

(sentence two in paragraph)

2. _____

_____

(sentence three in paragraph)

3. _____

_____

(sentence four in paragraph)

Use **START** to expand your ideas.

S Show colors, textures, tastes, and smells.

T Totally **describe** people, places, feelings, and emotions.

A Audience awareness: Does my audience understand my ideas?

R Reasons: Are there at least three "ideas" or "reasons" to explain my purpose?

T Tell specific details, such as numbers (sizes, dates, ages, time) and seasons.

④ **My Two-Minute Chat Partner Is:** _____

⑤ **Ending Sentence:** _____.

(sentence five in paragraph)

⑥ **Drafting:** Using printing paper, write your paragraph. First, copy your purpose sentence. Then, make a sentence out of each brain-storming idea. Finally, copy your ending sentence.

Following the Rainbow

GENRE: Fiction

SKILL: Sequencing—beginning, middle, and end

STANDARD: Use prewriting strategies to generate and organize ideas (e.g., focus on one topic; organize writing to include a beginning, middle, and end; use descriptive words when writing about people, places, things, and events).

ASSIGNMENT: Students will write a fictional story.

FOCUS: Tell students that they will again be working on a narrative paragraph. The last narrative was based on an actual event in their lives, but this one will be made up or imagined. This project, a fictional story, will be a little more difficult for some students.

Explain that narrative stories must follow a sequence, have a clear beginning, middle, and end, and use transitions that show the passing of time (see Week 26 Lesson). In addition, a good story fits together like a puzzle. If any of the pieces are missing, the story will not make sense.

MODEL: Read aloud a few St. Patrick's Day stories, such as *Clever Tom and the Leprechaun* by Linda Shute and *Jack and the Leprechaun* by Ivan Robertson. Discuss the themes of leprechauns, pots of gold, and rainbows in these stories. Also discuss the problem in each story, and how often characters make several unsuccessful attempts to solve a problem before they finally come to a resolution at the end. Then have students fold a paper into three rows and write the headings Beginning, Middle, and End at the top of each row. As you reread a story, allow students to draw a picture that represents the beginning, the middle, and the end of it.

Tell students that they will be writing their own story about a character who is looking for good fortune at the end of the rainbow. Students will invent a problem and at least one unsuccessful attempt to solve it before the final resolution.

PLANNING PAGE: The planning page for this project looks like a puzzle to remind students that a good story must fit together. Model how to generate characters, setting, a problem, and its solution on the planning page. Then hand out the story template (Appendix B, page 155) and model drafting a story with a beginning, middle, and end. As students draft independently, walk around and help as needed.

CONFERRING TIP

As students write drafts, they can be encouraged to turn each puzzle piece into a paragraph by adding sentences of elaboration. They will then have separate paragraphs about the characters, setting, problem, and solution. You can also point out similar paragraphs in their reading material.

Name: _____

Following the Rainbow

(1) **Analyzing the Audience:** The audience is your teacher and classmates. They do not know your story. Choose words that tell your story in order so that it makes sense to them.

(2) **Brainstorming:** Fill in the puzzle pieces to plan your story.

Characters Who is in your story?	**Setting** Where and when does the story take place?
_____ _____ _____ _____	_____ _____ _____
Problem What is it? How do the characters try to solve it?	**Solution** How was the problem solved?
_____ _____ _____	_____ _____ _____ _____

(3) **Drafting:** Use your puzzle to draft a story on the story template. Be sure your story has a beginning, middle, and end.

CHAPTER 10

April Writing Lessons

Daily Journal Prompts

**NATIONAL POETRY MONTH**

Be sure to read lots of poems and have students respond to them. Read a favorite and ask students to complete this prompt.

This poem reminded me of _____ .

Think about a time when you laughed very hard. What was it that was so funny?

I laughed so hard when _____ .

If you had the chance to ask your principal anything that you wanted, what would you ask?

If I could ask my principal anything, I'd ask him or her _____ .

As summer approaches, stores are filling their shelves with outside toys and warm-weather clothes. Think about one thing that you will be able to do in the summer.

In the summer, I will be able to _____ .

Think about all of the things that you did in school throughout the year. Which was your favorite? What did you learn while doing it?

The best thing that I did in school this year was _____ .

Our friends help make us happy. Think about a time when you made a friend happy. How did you feel when you made that friend happy?

I made my friend happy when _____ .

Write a detailed description of one exciting or interesting activity that you recently did. Include how you felt during the event or activity.

One exciting thing that I did recently was _____ .

What if there were no schools at all? What would your life be like?

If there were no schools, _____ .

No one likes to be sick, but sometimes sick days can be a nice break from the daily routine. What are some things that you can do if you take a sick day from school?

If I take a sick day from school, I can _____ .

EARTH DAY   We must all help to take care of Mother Earth. Write about one way that you could help Earth.

I could help Earth by _____ .

Pretend that you are telling an alien from outer space about pollution. How would you describe it so that they would understand what it is? Be specific. Remember—they probably do not know what garbage is or what automobiles are.

I would tell the alien that pollution is _____ .

What if we never recycled anything? What would our world be like?

If we never recycled anything, _____ .

Tell about something that you recently worked hard on. How did you feel about working so hard?

I recently worked hard on _____ .

Think about a time when someone helped you. Who was it that helped you? How did this person help?

Once somebody helped me by _____ .

Finish the following sentence with the first thought that comes to your mind. Then add more sentences to explain your thoughts.

I wish people would stop _____ .

Indoor vs. Outdoor Recess

GENRE: Persuasive paragraph

SKILL: Writing supporting sentences

STANDARD: Demonstrate focus, organization, and elaboration in writing. Write for a variety of purposes.

ASSIGNMENT: Students will write a persuasive paragraph to convince their teacher and principal that indoor or outdoor recess is better.

FOCUS: Recall with students the persuasive sentences that they wrote in October (page 58) and the persuasive letter that they wrote in March (page 112). Explain that they will be writing a persuasive paragraph with the goal of convincing the audience—the teacher, the principal, and their classmates—that their school should have outdoor or indoor recess.

Students must first decide which recess they would like to have. Put students in pairs and have them take turns supporting each side. For the first two to three minutes, one student argues for indoor recess while the other supports outdoor; then they switch. After this exercise, each student must decide which recess they will write about. Remind students that supporting sentences must support the purpose statement. If a sentence does not support the purpose statement, it should be deleted. Their ending sentence should be powerful and restate their recess choice.

MODEL: Model some sample paragraphs with supporting sentences that do not belong and invite students to find these sentences.

> I think that we should have outside recess. We need to be able to get exercise by running across the field and playing kickball games. Breathing in the fresh air helps to keep us healthy. Once my sister couldn't go outside because she had a cold. The fresh air helps to clear our minds so that we can learn new things. Also, it would be a terrible waste not to be able to use our new jungle gym. Outside recess is the only choice for students at Edison School!

PLANNING PAGE: Distribute the Indoor vs. Outdoor Recess Planning Page. Read and discuss the steps. After each step, model it, and then pause to allow students to complete that step.

CONFERRING TIP

Some students may have trouble determining which side they feel more strongly about. If this is the case, help them to create a pro and con list for each alternative; tell them that after brainstorming, the list with the most pros (and least cons) is most likely the side they feel more strongly about and should therefore argue for, ensuring a heartfelt essay, which is much easier to compose.

Name: _____

Indoor vs. Outdoor Recess

1. **Analyzing the Audience:** The audience is your teacher, principal, and classmates. They may or may not share your feelings.

2. **Setting the Purpose:** Our school should have indoor/outdoor recess because _____.

   (sentence one in paragraph)

3. **Brainstorming:** List three (3) reasons for your choice. Remember that you are trying to convince people to think the same way that you do.

   1. _____
      _____

      (sentence two in paragraph)

   2. _____
      _____

      (sentence three in paragraph)

   3. _____
      _____

      (sentence four in paragraph)

   Use **START** to expand your ideas.

   S Show colors, textures, tastes, and smells.

   T Totally describe people, places, feelings, and emotions.

   A Audience awareness: Does my audience understand my ideas?

   R Reasons: Are there at least three "ideas" or "reasons" to explain my purpose?

   T Tell specific details, such as numbers (sizes, dates, ages, time) and seasons.

4. **My Two-Minute Chat Partner Is:** _____

5. **Ending Sentence:** _____.

   (sentence five in paragraph)

6. **Drafting:** Using printing paper, write your paragraph. First, copy your purpose sentence. Then, make a sentence out of each reason. Finally, copy your ending sentence.

Grade 1 Writing Curriculum: Week-by-Week Lessons Scholastic Teaching Resources

Rainy-Day Fun

GENRE: Expository paragraph

SKILL: Using time-order transitions

STANDARD: Communicate ideas in writing to accomplish a variety
            of purposes.

ASSIGNMENT: Students will write an expository paragraph about something
            that can be done on a rainy day.

FOCUS: Ask students to think of a time when a rainy day spoiled their fun. Share some examples of times when plans had to be changed due to rainy weather. Invite students to think of some activities that can be fun to do on a rainy day, so that they will be prepared the next time a storm rushes in.

MODEL: Make a list of activities on the chalkboard, overhead, or chart paper. Ask students to choose one of the activities mentioned or one of their own. Students should then write step-by-step directions for the activity using time-order transitions; see the list at right.

after	again
at last	before
during	first
from then on	in the meantime
lastly	meanwhile
soon	when
afterward	as
at the same time	best of all
finally	first of all
immediately	last of all
later on	next
then	while

   To illustrate just how carefully they must think as they write their directions, ask them to follow these directions for getting a drink of water:

> First, line up at the front door. Then, quietly walk down the hall to the drinking fountain. When you reach the fountain, line up against the wall and wait patiently. Finally, walk back to the classroom quietly.

   If students follow the directions carefully, they will notice that getting the actual drink was not in the directions!

PLANNING PAGE: Distribute the Rainy-Day Fun Planning Page. Read and discuss the following steps: Analyzing the Audience, Setting the Purpose, Brainstorming, and Drafting. After each step, model it, and then pause to allow students to complete that step. Have the students list in the margins the transitions they will use.

CONFERRING TIP

Transitions are often followed by a comma. Help the students to identify when to use a comma.

Rainy-Day Fun

Name: _____

(1) **Analyzing the Audience:** Teacher and classmates. They may or may not be familiar with the activity that you are explaining.

(2) **Setting the Purpose:** A fun thing to do on a rainy day is

_____.

(sentence one in paragraph)

(3) **Brainstorming:** List the steps involved in your activity. Remember that someone must be able to follow your directions. Use the back if you have more steps.

1. _____

_____

(sentence two in paragraph)

2. _____

_____

(sentence three in paragraph)

3. _____

_____

(sentence four in paragraph)

Use **START** to expand your ideas.

S Show colors, textures, tastes, and smells.

T Totally describe people, places, feelings, and emotions.

A Audience awareness: Does my audience understand my ideas?

R Reasons: Are there at least three "ideas" or "reasons" to explain my purpose?

T Tell specific details, such as numbers (sizes, dates, ages, time) and seasons.

(4) **My Two-Minute Chat Partner Is:** _____

(5) **Ending Sentence:** _____.

(sentence five in paragraph)

(6) **Drafting:** Using printing paper, write your paragraph. First, copy your purpose sentence. Then, make a sentence out of each brainstorming idea. Finally, copy your ending sentence.

Grade 1 Writing Curriculum: Week-by-Week Lessons Scholastic Teaching Resources

Who Let the Dog Out?

GENRE: Fiction

SKILL: Using rich vocabulary

STANDARD: Relate character, setting, and plot to real-life situations.

ASSIGNMENT: Students will write a creative story.

FOCUS: The focus of this assignment will be to show students how rich vocabulary can help paint a clear picture in the readers' minds. Recall the planning puzzle that was used last month (see page 118). Remind students that a good story fits together like a puzzle. If any one of the pieces is missing, the story will not make sense. Students will again use the puzzle organizer to plan their story. This time, however, the problem/conflict is given: *One day I walked into the yard and noticed that my dog was missing.* Students need to decide what events led up to the problem and how this problem was solved.

MODEL: Use the following example or one of your own to begin illustrating rich vocabulary.

> When I noticed that my dog was missing, I went to tell my mom.

Explain to students that this sentence gives important information, but it is hard to picture in our minds. Was the character in a hurry to tell Mom? Did he or she run? Are there any other ways we can say *run* that will show us even more? Did the character *dash*, *race*, *sprint*, or even *fly*? These words all tell the reader that the character was in a hurry to get Mom because this was an emergency.

Encourage students to choose rich, colorful words that will help paint a picture in the minds of the readers. Some students will be able to put them in as they draft, while other students will need to be encouraged to add them during the editing process.

PLANNING PAGE: Distribute the Who Let the Dog Out? Planning Page, which has the puzzle graphic organizer. In this case, the problem is already entered, but students must choose the characters, setting, events, and solution. Walk them through this step. Then distribute the story template (Appendix B, page 155) and model drafting a story with a beginning, middle, and end. As students draft independently, walk around and help as needed.

CONFERRING TIP

Troubleshoot with those who are struggling with the puzzle graphic organizer by creating a list from which they can choose. For example:

Characters: Mom, Sister, Mailman, Bobby, Kailey, Garbage Collector, Dad, George

Settings: house in the city, house in the country, farmhouse, house in the mountains, rainy day, sunny day, blustery winter day

Problems: dog went to the park, dog hopped on the garbage truck, Mom left the gate open, someone stole the dog, dog ran after the ice-cream truck

Solutions: Neighbor brought the dog home, police brought the dog home because he had his address on his tags, we found him in the park

Name: _____

Who Let the Dog Out?

(1) **Analyzing the Audience:** The audience is your teacher and classmates. They do not know what event led up to the problem and how the problem is solved in your story. Remember to choose words that will paint a picture in their minds.

(2) **Brainstorming:** Fill in the puzzle pieces to plan your story.

Characters Who is in your story?	**Setting** Where and when does the story take place?
_____ _____ _____ _____	_____ _____ _____
Problem One day, I walked into the yard and noticed that my dog was missing. _____ _____ _____	**Solution** How was the problem solved? _____ _____ _____

(3) **Drafting:** Use your puzzle to draft a story on the story template. Be sure your story has a beginning, middle, and end.

Grade 1 Writing Curriculum: Week-by-Week Lessons Scholastic Teaching Resources

May Writing Lessons

Daily Journal Prompts

You have many special qualities. Perhaps you are a good listener or a hard worker. Think about all of your special qualities. Which do you think is the best?

The best thing about me is _____ .

All families are special and unique. They have different customs and traditions. What do you like best about your family?

The best thing about my family is _____ .

Write a detailed description of one exciting or interesting activity that you recently did. Include how you felt during the activity.

One exciting thing that I did recently was _____ .

There are probably some things that you like about school, as well as some things that you don't like about school. How could school be better for you?

School would be better if _____ .

Think about something that you are good at doing. How would you teach someone else to do it?

I could teach someone how to _____ .

We all have things that we worry about. What is something that worries you? Why do you worry about it?

Something that I worry about is _____ .

PARENTS' DAY   What do you love most about you parent(s)?

The thing that I love most about my parent(s) is _____

_____ .

How would your parent(s) describe you?

My parent(s) would describe me as _____ .

What would you like/hate most about being a parent?

If I were a parent, I would like/hate _____

_____ .

Tell what your parent(s) do to make you laugh.

My _____

makes me laugh by _____ .

Describe a present that you would like to give to your mom or your dad and tell why you would like to give it to him/her.

I would like to give my _____

a _____ .

Describe the best birthday gift you've ever received. When did you receive it? Who gave it to you? How did you feel when you got it?

The best birthday gift I ever received was _____ .

What would you do if only one hot dog was left and neither you nor your friend had had one?

If there was only one hot dog left, I would _____ .

As summer approaches, we start to think about outside activities. Would you like a built-in pool in your yard? Give reasons for your answer.

I would/would not like a built-in pool in my yard because _____ .

Which do you think is better to ride: a scooter or a bicycle? Give reasons for your answer.

A scooter/bicycle is better to ride because _____ .

Convince your parents that all children do or do not need a computer. Be sure to give reasons that will convince them of your belief.

All students do/do not need a computer because _____.

MEMORIAL DAY Who is your hero or heroine and why?

My hero/heroine is _____

because _____.

Describe the qualities that make a hero/heroine.

The qualities that a hero/heroine should have are _____.

_____.

Describe your life as a caterpillar. Think about what you know about the life cycle of a butterfly.

My life as a caterpillar would be _____.

_____.

Describe the worst rainstorm you have ever seen. Were you inside or outside during the storm? How did you feel during the storm?

The worst rainstorm was _____

_____.

Taking Care of a Pet

GENRE: Expository paragraph

SKILL: Editing/revising

STANDARD: Use correct grammar, spelling, punctuation, capitalization, and structure.

ASSIGNMENT: Students will compose an expository paragraph explaining how to take care of a pet.

FOCUS: Begin a discussion about pets and what a responsibility it is to have them. Ask students to share stories about their own pets, and tell them they'll be writing a paragraph explaining how to take care of a pet. If students don't have pets, ask them to imagine what it would be like.

MODEL: Most of the students should feel fairly comfortable with paragraph writing at this point. While you will continue to conference with them about their work, it is time to give them more ownership of the editing/revising process.

Make a poster of STOP (Appendix D, page 157). Demonstrate how to check each step on a sample paragraph you've prepared. You may even want to make an individual checklist of the acronym that students can check off as they revise.

PLANNING PAGE: Distribute the Taking Care of a Pet Planning Page. Read and discuss the following steps: Analyzing the Audience, Setting the Purpose, Brainstorming, and Drafting. At this point, you can allow the students to work through it alone.

CONFERRING TIP

Be sure to focus on only one or two grammatical items, as more than that is overwhelming.

STOP:

S **Spelling:** Did I spell the words as best I can by sounding them out and using word banks and word walls? Did I use the dictionary?

T **Tells the purpose:** Does my first sentence communicate the purpose of my writing?

O **Organization and Out loud:** How does my paragraph sound when I read it aloud? Are there any parts that do not make sense, do not flow, or just sound funny? If so, could this be a grammar or punctuation error?

P **Punctuation and capitalization:** Did I use proper punctuation and capitalization?

Name: _____

Taking Care of a Pet

(1) **Analyzing the Audience:** The audience is your teacher and class-mates. They may or may not know how to care for the pet.

(2) **Setting the Purpose:** Taking care of a _____
is a big responsibility.   (sentence one in paragraph)

(3) **Brainstorming:** List three things that you must do to take care of this pet. Try to put them in order from greatest to least importance.

1. _____

_____

(sentence two in paragraph)

2. _____

_____

(sentence three in paragraph)

3. _____

_____

(sentence four in paragraph)

Use **START** to expand your ideas.

S Show colors, textures, tastes, and smells.

T Totally **describe** people, places, feelings, and emotions.

A Audience awareness: Does my audience understand my ideas?

R Reasons: Are there at least three "ideas" or "reasons" to explain my purpose?

T Tell specific details, such as numbers (sizes, dates, ages, time) and seasons.

(4) **My Two-Minute Chat Partner Is:** _____

(5) **Ending Sentence:** _____.
                                              (sentence five in paragraph)

(6) **Drafting:** Using printing paper, write your paragraph. Use STOP to revise and edit your paragraph.

Grade 1 Writing Curriculum: Week-by-Week Lessons Scholastic Teaching Resources

When I Was a Baby

GENRE: Narrative paragraph

SKILL: Understanding subject-verb agreement and past-tense verb formation

STANDARD: Use correct grammar, spelling, punctuation, capitalization, and structure.

ASSIGNMENT: Students will write a paragraph telling about something that they did when they were babies.

FOCUS: Ask students to tell stories about what they did when they were babies. You may want to ask them to bring in baby pictures or share some of your own. After students share some stories, tell them that this week they'll be writing about something they did when they were babies. (If students can't think of anything, have them ask their parents.)

MODEL: Now that your students are comfortable with the writing process, you'll want to focus your efforts on some common grammatical errors. Forming past-tense verbs and making subjects and verbs agree are two problems young writers commonly have. Since students are writing this week about events that happened in the past, it's a perfect time to address these issues.

Point out to students that they'll be writing this story in the past tense, since they'll be describing events that happened long ago. Following are some rules to share with your students about the proper use of verbs. You may wish to make posters reminding students of these rules or create mini-lessons to give which students can get extra practice. Choose an area to focus on based on your assessment of students' needs. Demonstrate as you write about something you did as a child.

- Past-tense verbs tell about actions that already happened. Many past-tense verbs end in -ed. If a verb already ends in -e, just add -d.

  I jumped on my trampoline.

  I liked when I visited my grandma's house.

CONFERRING TIP

Have students read their work aloud to you. Often students can hear their errors when read aloud; they can recognize language that sounds funny.

- Irregular verbs become different words when used in the past tense.

  Examples: <u>present</u>   <u>past</u>

present	past
is	was
do	did
begin	began
run	ran
sleep	slept
throw	threw
tell	told
wear	wore

- Sentences must have subject-verb agreement. A noun or pronoun is usually the subject of the sentence. The subject can be singular or plural.

- Singular subjects need singular verbs. Singular, present-tense verbs end in -s.

  Sarah plays in the band.

- Plural subjects need plural verbs. Plural, present-tense verbs do not end in -s.

  Sarah and Jack play in the band.

PRACTICE: Have the students correct the following example for past-tense verb errors and subject-verb agreement errors.

> When I is a baby I sleeped a lot. I weared onesies and play-clothes all day. My sister and I plays a little with the jungle gym, but I mostly liked to sleeps. I still have the first pajamas I weared, and I still loves to sleep like a baby.

PLANNING PAGE: Distribute the When I Was a Baby Planning Page. Read and discuss the following steps: Analyzing the Audience, Setting the Purpose, Brainstorming, and Drafting. At this point, you can allow the students to work through it alone.

Name: _____

When I Was a Baby

(1) **Analyzing the Audience:** Teacher and classmates. They do not know the funny things that you did when you were a baby.

(2) **Setting the Purpose:** When I was a baby I used to

_____.

(sentence one in paragraph)

(3) **Brainstorming:** List three ideas about your purpose.

1. _____

   _____

   (sentence two in paragraph)

2. _____

   _____

   (sentence three in paragraph)

3. _____

   _____

   (sentence four in paragraph)

Use **START** to expand your ideas.

S Show colors, textures, tastes, and smells.

T Totally **describe** people, places, feelings, and emotions.

A Audience awareness: Does my audience understand my ideas?

R Reasons: Are there at least three "ideas" or "reasons" to explain my purpose?

T Tell specific details, such as numbers (sizes, dates, ages, time) and seasons.

(4) **My Two-Minute Chat Partner Is:** _____

(5) **Ending Sentence:** _____.

(sentence five in paragraph)

(6) **Drafting:** Write your paragraph on printing paper. Use STOP to revise and edit your paragraph.

Earning a Privilege

GENRE: Persuasive paragraph

SKILL: Choosing titles

STANDARD: Communicate ideas in writing to accomplish a variety of purposes.

ASSIGNMENT: Students will write a persuasive paragraph to try to earn a privilege.

FOCUS: Begin a discussion of privileges, asking students to share some that they have, both at home and in the classroom. Ensure that all students understand what a privilege is—a special thing they get to do because of their age or responsible behavior. Let students know that people must earn privileges. Ask them to think about privileges they believe they are ready for. Tell them that this week they'll get to write a persuasive paragraph to convince an adult that they are ready for a new privilege.

MODEL: Before getting into the brainstorming on the planning page, introduce the skill for the week: choosing titles. While the writing assignments have been titled for organizational purposes, we have not, as yet, talked about students choosing titles for their work. Students are often quick to title their writing, long before it has been completed. When this happens, the original title often does not capture the main idea of the text. Sometimes students feel constrained by the title and limit their writing to fit. This week, the strategy is to title a piece after it has been completed.

Ask students why writers give titles to their stories. How do titles help readers? To model their importance, you might want to try omitting the titles of read-alouds, or substituting very boring ones. When you finish reading, ask students to volunteer titles that would and would not suit the story. Then ask students how they think authors come up with titles. Guide them to understand that writers often title stories when they've finished writing; if they title a story first, the story might change during the writing process, and the title might not be right anymore. Tell students that this week they will give their paragraph a title after they finish writing it.

PLANNING PAGE: Distribute the Earning a Privilege Planning Page. Read and discuss the following steps: Analyzing the Audience, Setting the Purpose, Brainstorming, and Drafting. At this point, you can allow the students to work through it alone.

CONFERRING TIP

Do not hesitate to use the thesaurus when brainstorming for a title together.

Name: _____

Earning a Privilege

(1) **Analyzing the Audience:** The audience is an adult who may or may not agree that you deserve the privilege.

(2) **Setting the Purpose:** One privilege that I deserve is

_____.

(sentence one in paragraph)

(3) **Brainstorming:** List three reasons why you feel that you deserve the privilege. Remember that you are trying to convince people that you deserve this privilege.

1. _____

_____

(sentence two in paragraph)

2. _____

_____

(sentence three in paragraph)

3. _____

_____

(sentence four in paragraph)

Use **START** to expand your ideas.

S Show colors, textures, tastes, and smells.

T Totally **describe** people, places, feelings, and emotions.

A Audience awareness: Does my audience understand my ideas?

R Reasons: Are there at least three "ideas" or "reasons" to explain my purpose?

T Tell specific details, such as numbers (sizes, dates, ages, time) and seasons.

(4) **My Two-Minute Chat Partner Is:** _____

(5) **Ending Sentence:** _____.

(sentence five in paragraph)

(6) **Drafting:** Using printing paper, write your paragraph. Use STOP to revise and edit your paragraph. Then give it a title.

A New Take on an Old Story

GENRE: Fiction

SKILL: Using dialogue

STANDARD: Identify how the author and illustrators express their ideas

ASSIGNMENT: Students will write a story, based on a familiar story.

FOCUS: Explain to students that they are going to write their own story using a favorite read-aloud as a model. They can change the characters, setting, problem, solution, and details. For example, Little Red Riding Hood can become Little White Parka Hood. The setting can be the Arctic tundra, and a polar bear can confront Little White Parka Hood.

Reread the original story and invite students to discuss how they might change it.

MODEL: Tell students that when they write their stories, they should use dialogue, having characters talk to each other. Explain that authors use marks called quotation marks to make dialogue clear to readers. To teach students about quotation marks, ask them to go on a hunt and locate some quotation marks in their reading books. Point out that these marks are put around the exact words that a character says:

> "Let me go!" screamed Little Red Riding Hood.

Make it clear that "screamed Little Red Riding Hood" does not need to be inside the quotation marks because she did not say those words.

Each time a new character speaks, remind students that it is a new paragraph. Point out examples of this in books.

As students write their stories, encourage them to use a yellow marker to highlight the words spoken by characters. They can then go back and put quotation marks around these highlighted words.

PLANNING PAGE: Distribute the A New Take on an Old Story Planning Page, which has the puzzle graphic organizer. Model completing it with alternate characters, setting, problem, and solution from the read-aloud. Have students do the same. Distribute the story template (Appendix B, page 155) and invite students to draft a story with a beginning, middle, and end.

CONFERRING

f students are struggling with altering the story features, help them create a new character, setting, and problem. They can then elaborate and fill in the solution and details.

Name: _____

A New Take on an Old Story

1 **Analyzing the Audience:** The audience is your teacher and classmates. They know the story that you are using for a model, but they do not know your changes.

2 **Brainstorming:** Fill in the puzzle pieces to plan your story.

Characters
Who is in your story?

_____

_____

_____

_____

Setting
Where and when does the story take place?

_____

_____

_____

Problem
What happened? Tell three exciting events.

_____

_____

_____

Solution
How was the problem solved?

_____

_____

_____

_____

3 **Drafting:** Use your story puzzle to draft your story on the story template. Be sure your story has a beginning, middle, and end.

Grade 1 Writing Curriculum: Week-by-Week Lessons Scholastic Teaching Resources

CHAPTER 12

June Writing Lessons

Daily Journal Prompts

Describe your favorite thing to do over the summer.

My favorite thing to do over the summer is _____ .

How would you describe your classroom to the students who will be in it next year? What are some things that you think they'll like about it?

Room # _____ *is* _____ .

You have been given 3 marbles: blue, orange, and red. Create a game for yourself or for you and a friend to play.

My marble game is _____ .

Write a detailed description of one exciting or interesting activity that you recently did. Include how you felt during the activity.

One exciting thing that I did recently was _____ .

If you could paint your bedroom today, what color would you paint it and why?

I would paint my bedroom _____ .

Pretend that you are a squirrel. Describe your life.

My life as a squirrel is _____.

Pretend that you are a kite floating through the air. Where would you like to fly and why?

If I were a kite, I would like to fly to _____.

Describe a fun day at the beach. Include your feelings.

My fun day at the beach would include _____.

Write a letter to next years' teacher describing yourself and what you want to learn.

Next year I want to learn _____.

Think about your favorite sport. Do you like to play it, or do you like to watch it? What makes it your favorite?

My favorite sport is _____

because _____.

Describe a good teacher.

A good teacher _____ .

Pretend that you are a frog catching dinner. Describe your hunt.

If I were a frog hunting for dinner, I would _____ .

You have been chosen to plan the class field trip. Where are you going? When are you going, and why did you choose this spot?

For the class field trip, we will _____ .

Describe a toy or an action figure that you would like to make. What would it look like? Would it do anything special?

A toy or action figure that I would like to make is _____ .

If you had the chance to tell next year's teacher something about yourself, what would it be?

I would tell my future teacher _____ .

Acrostic Poem

GENRE: Poetry

SKILL: Using descriptive language

STANDARD: Describe differences between prose and poetry.

ASSIGNMENT: Students will write an acrostic poem.

FOCUS: This month's writing focus is on poetry. Students have heard and read poetry throughout the year; now they can try their hand at writing it. The poetic forms introduced this month are highly structured and do not all require rhyme, which helps students feel successful at writing poetry and builds their confidence in working with this genre.

Begin with the question, "What is a poem?" Most young students will tell you that a poem is something that rhymes. Point out that not all poems rhyme. Describe the differences between poetry and prose. Poetry expresses a strong feeling about one topic. It is usually much shorter than prose, often only a few lines. Lines can contain anywhere from one word to a complete sentence, and one sentence can be broken up over several lines. Discuss the idea that because poetry is short, it is crucial that the imagery be bold and appeal to the senses.

When working on poetry now as well as during poetry month (April), immerse your students in the genre. Share your own poems, choose from anthologies found in the library, or select from reading textbooks. Some good resources include *A Child's Book of Poems* (Backpack Books), *Favorite Poems, Old and New*, selected by Helen Ferris (Bantam Doubleday Dell), and *A Child's Garden of Verses*, by Robert Louis Stevenson (Chronicle Books).

Reread poems at least twice when sharing them, and encourage students to read their own poems aloud multiple times as they write.

Tell students that the first poem they'll write is called an acrostic poem. An acrostic poem is a poem in which the first letters of each line form a word when read vertically.

TIP

Read aloud lots of poetry this month so students can get a feel for the genre. You can share your own favorites and those from your textbook.

MODEL: As a group, select a topic word, preferably an animal or season. Write this word vertically on chart paper, the chalkboard, or the overhead. Brainstorm words and phrases that begin with each letter and relate to the topic. Remind students to think of the five senses and imagery as they choose words for the poem. Assure them that the poem does not have to rhyme, but it should sound pleasing and create pictures in the reader's mind.

Here are two examples of acrostic poems.

FALL

Falling on the piles
Around the yard, they blow.
Lovely crimson colors
Leaves all aglow.

CAT

Climbed through the window
Another night of adventure
Tree after tree, while *my* owner looks for me.

PLANNING PAGE: Distribute the Acrostic Poem Planning Page, and walk the students through writing the poem. Have students brainstorm words and phrases that begin with the letters in their word. Be sure to review the model poem the next day as they begin to choose words and draft the poem.

CONFERRING TIP

Poetry is about strong emotion or passion for something. If some students are having trouble, encourage them to choose another topic—something for which they have strong feelings.

Name: _____

Acrostic Poem

(1) **Choose** an animal or season you really love and write the word vertically on the lines below.

(2) **Brainstorm** words and phrases that begin with each letter of the word and relate to the topic. Write them on the lines beside the letters. Use the back if you need more room.

_____

_____

_____

_____

_____

_____

_____

(3) **Draft:** To draft the poem, write your word vertically on another sheet of paper. Choose words from your brainstorm above to create descriptive phrases and sentences about your topic.

(4) **Revise:** After you confer with your teacher, revise your poem and illustrate it. Remember: if you have replacement or additional words, it is okay to add them as you revise.

Grade 1 Writing Curriculum: Week-by-Week Lessons Scholastic Teaching Resources

Name Poem

GENRE: Poetry

SKILL: Rhyming words

STANDARD: Communicate ideas in writing to accomplish a variety of purposes.

ASSIGNMENT: Students will write a name poem, using their name and including two words that rhyme.

FOCUS: Tell the students that they have already written an acrostic poem, one that did not have to rhyme. They will be excited to know that for the next poem, they will again write an acrostic, but this time they will use their name and a minimum of two words that rhyme.

MODEL: You can use your name to model. First, write your name vertically on the overhead, chalkboard, or chart paper. Then brainstorm words that begin with each letter of your name and describe something about you and, when possible, rhyme. Point out that many rhyming words come from the same word families and have common spelling patterns.

Example:

M mighty, merry, mother

A art, articulate

R running, roaring,

Y yard, yo-yo

Using your brainstormed words, draft the rhyming poem.

Example:

Mighty merry mother of two

Always looking for something to do, from

Running, gardening, swimming, and skiing to

Yo-yoing and painting, always looking after the happiness of her crew.

CONFERRING TIP

Some students may have trouble brainstorming and using rhyming words. Allow them to brainstorm and draft the poem without rhyming words, and make this the last focus; once they have words to work with, they can then attempt to find rhyming words. You can invite the whole class to help find rhyming words.

Note how we added and deleted words through the drafting phase; allow students to see you do this as a normal part of writing. Also, note that it does not matter where the rhymes occur within the poem. Give students time to illustrate and share their poetry with others. You may even wish to create a class poetry book.

PLANNING PAGE: Distribute the Name Poem Planning Page and walk students through the steps. Remind students that poetry is to be read aloud, so when they are brainstorming and revising, you should hear them reading aloud. The final draft should be done the following day.

Name: _____

Name Poem

① **Write** your name vertically on the lines below.

② **Brainstorm** words and phrases that begin with each letter of your name and that describe who you are. Write them on the lines beside the letters.

_____

_____

_____

_____

_____

_____

_____

③ **Draft:** Write your name vertically on another sheet of paper. Choose words from your brainstorm above to create descriptive phrases and sentences about yourself. Try to include one rhyming word pair.

④ **Revise:** After you confer with your teacher, revise your poem and illustrate it. Remember: if you have replacement or additional words, it is okay to add them as you revise.

Grade 1 Writing Curriculum: Week-by-Week Lessons Scholastic Teaching Resources

Cinquain

GENRE: Poetry

SKILL: Using descriptive language

STANDARD: Communicate ideas in writing to accomplish a variety of purposes.

ASSIGNMENT: Students will write a cinquain.

FOCUS: Tell students that this week they'll try out a new kind of poem called a cinquain. The verse in a cinquain does not rhyme; however, it does follow a very specific set of rules.

Line 1   One word (title or subject)

Line 2   Two words (describes the title or subject)

Line 3   Three words (describes an action related to the title or subject)

Line 4   Four words (describes a feeling about the subject or title)

Line 5   One word (refers back to the title—can be the same word as the title or another word that refers to it)

MODEL: Model writing some cinquains with the class before you send them off on their own. Be sure to let them illustrate and share their final products.

Baby	Dog
Soft, gentle	Loving pet
Cries for mom	Watches over us
Loves to be fed	A man's best friend
Infant	Wags

PLANNING PAGE: Distribute the Cinquain Planning Page and the Cinquain template (on page 153) and walk the students through the steps, using the sample for further explanation. Be sure to build in another day for the final draft.

CONFERRING TIP

Some students have a very hard time not writing in complete sentences. In this case, have them write one sentence per line, and then help them to pull out the strongest word/words for the poem, eliminating the weak words, such as the helping verbs (*is, are, was*). Here's an example:

Riding a Scooter:

Riding a scooter is a cross between a bicycle and a skateboard.

It is swishing and kicking across the ground.

The scooter is whipping around corners and speeding across the floor.

I love the freedom of quickly racing around.

Now here is the completed cinquain:

Scootering

Bicycling, skateboarding

Swishing, kicking, whipping freedom, roaming, love, racing Motoring

Name: _____

Cinquain

A cinquain is a five-line poem. See the sample cinquain on the right.

(**1**) Choose a topic (which is also your title) for your cinquain.

_____

(**2**) Draw a picture of your topic to help you describe it.

> **Sample Cinquain**
>
> Summer
> Sun, fun
> Swimming, running, climbing,
> Warmth, relaxation, happiness, healing
> Sensational

[drawing box]

(**3**) Fill in the cinquain template.

(**4**) **To Be Completed the Next Day:** Write the poem on a new sheet of paper. Remember that it is okay to change or add words. Be sure to also illustrate your poem.

Cinquain Template

Line 1: the title

_____

(one word)

Line 2: describe the title

_____ _____

(two words)

Line 3 : describe an action

_____ _____ _____

(three words)

Line 4: describe a feeling about the topic

_____ _____

_____ _____

(four words)

Line 5: refer back to the title

_____

(one word)

_____ (date)

Dear_____,
        (greeting)

(body)

Write your Setting the Purpose sentence from the planning page:

_____

_____

Use your planning page to write sentences with each of your three brainstorming ideas, and conclude with your ending sentence:

_____

_____

_____

_____

_____

Love,

_____

Your Name
(closing)

Grade 1 Writing Curriculum: Week-by-Week Lessons Scholastic Teaching Resources

Name: _____ **Date:** _____

The Beginning: In the beginning of the story, describe the setting and introduce the characters and the problem. What happens in the beginning of your story?

_____

_____

_____

_____

The Middle: In the middle of a story, the characters try to solve the problem. Often their first try doesn't work, and they have to try something else. What happens in the middle of your story?

_____

_____

_____

_____

The End: In the end of a story, the problem is solved. What happens in the end of your story?

_____

_____

_____

_____

Time-Order Transitions

after	immediately
afterward	in the meantime
again	last
at last	lastly
at the same time	last of all
before	later on
best of all	meanwhile
during	next
fifth	second
finally	soon
first	then
first of all	third
from then on	when
fourth	while

Grade 1 Writing Curriculum: Week-by-Week Lessons Scholastic Teaching Resources

Student Page

STOP:

S **Spelling:** Did I spell the words as best as I can by sounding them out and using word banks and word walls? Did I use the dictionary?

T **Tells the purpose:** Does my first sentence communicate the purpose of my writing?

O **Organization and Out loud:** How does my paragraph sound when I read it aloud? Are there any parts that do not make sense, do not flow, or just sound funny? If so, could this be a grammar or punctuation error?

P **Punctuation and capitalization:** Did I use proper punctuation and capitalization?

Student Page

START:

S **Show** colors, textures, tastes, and smells.

T **Totally** describe people, places, feelings, and emotions.

A **Audience awareness:** Does my audience understand my ideas?

R **Reasons:** Are there at least three "ideas" or "reasons" to explain my purpose?

T **Tell** specific details, such as numbers (size, dates, ages, time) and seasons.

Name: _____ **Date:** _____

Writing Checklist: Sentences

☐ **yes** ☐ **no** Did I begin with my purpose statement?

☐ **yes** ☐ **no** Did I add detail by making sentences out of my key words?

☐ **yes** ☐ **no** Did I use proper punctuation and capitalization in my sentences?

☐ **yes** ☐ **no** Does my writing make sense?

Name: _____ Date: _____

Writing Checklist: Paragraphs

yes   no   Do I have 5 sentences?

yes   no   Did I begin with my purpose statement?

yes   no   Did I add detail by making sentences out of my key words?

yes   no   Did I use proper punctuation and capitalization in my sentences?

Recommended Reading

Anson, Charles M. *Writing and Response*. Urbana, IL: NCTE, 1989.

Calkins, Lucy McCormick. *The Art of Teaching Writing*. Portsmouth, NH: Heinemann, 1994.

Cohen, Moshe, and Margaret Riel. "The Effects of Distant Audiences on Students' Writing." *American Educational Research Journal*. 26.2 (Sum. 1989): 143-159.

Cooper, Charles R. and Lee Odell, eds. *Evaluating Writing: Describing, Measuring, Judging*. Urbana, IL: NCTE, 1977

Elbow, Peter. *Writing Without Teachers*. New York: Oxford UP, 1973.

Elbow, Peter and Pat Belanoff. *Sharing and Responding*. New York: Random House, 1989.

Graves, Donald. *A Fresh Look At Writing*. Portsmouth, NH: Heinemann, 1994.

Hillocks, G., Jr. & Smith, M.W. "Grammars and literacy learning." In J. Flood, D. Lapp, J.R. Squire, & J.M. Jensen (Eds.), *Handbook of Research on Teaching the English Language Arts* (2nd ed.). Mahwah, NJ: Erlbaum, 2003.

Hillocks, G. Jr. "Research on written composition: New Directions for teaching." Urbana, IL: National Conference on Research in English/ERIC Clearinghouse on Reading and Communication Skills, 1986.

Lees, Elaine O. "Evaluating Student Writing." *College Composition and Communication*. 30.4 (Dec. 1979): 370-74.

Odell, Lee. "The Process of Writing and the Process of Learning." *College Composition and Communication*. 31.1 (Feb. 1980): 42-50.

Tate, Gary and Edward P.J. Corbett, eds. *The Writing Teacher's Sourcebook*. New York: Oxford UP, 1981.

Weaver, Constance. *Understanding Whole Language*. Portsmouth, NH: Heinemann, 1990.